CUCINA
NAPOLETANA

CUCINA NAPOLETANA

100 RECIPES FROM ITALY'S MOST VIBRANT CITY

ARTURO IENGO

IN ASSOCIATION WITH I.R.V.A.T.

NAPLES PHOTOGRAPHY BY HANNAH MORNEMENT

INTERLINK BOOKS
An imprint of Interlink Publishing Group, Inc.

CONTENTS

INTRODUCTION

With more than 300 miles of wonderful coastline, two national parks, a vast plain, and spellbinding mountain landscapes, Campania is a rich and diverse region offering all the variety you can imagine.

The long history of this region has left a deep mark on the archaeology, the monuments, the secular and religious architecture, the character of its people, and on the warm hospitality that always amazes first-time visitors to Campania. It's the ancient land where Ulysses and Aeneas roamed, a land of myths and enchanting mermaids. A land which has been lived in and loved by great artists, whose creative genius can be recognized in the architecture, sculptures, and paintings in which the region is so rich. A land to be visited and discovered – from the traditional crafts of its artisans to its characteristic produce, from its distinctive wines to its lively cuisine, and to the songs and music that crossed over the boundaries of the region to conquer the entire world. The ancient Greeks and Romans, the Arabs, the Spanish, and the French have all left their mark on this part of the world that has so many traditions of its own to offer.

Campania needs to be enjoyed from village to village, from local tradition to local tradition, and from corner to corner to appreciate the full range of the land and all it has to offer. Take your pick from the wonderful islands, the enchanted coastlines, the engaging vistas of mountains, rivers, and lakes – every twist in the road or turning of a corner seems to offer a unique sight or a new experience to explore, all within easy reach.

The history of the region has also left an indelible mark on the cuisine. Innate appreciation of fresh produce and economical treatment of food are woven into the very fabric of daily and cultural life. *Cucina povera*, or poor man's food, is a prime example of this, where fresh ingredients are used in simple but flavorful combinations to make the most of what is on hand. Fresh vegetables, pasta, legumes, and seafood dominate, with very little meat in most of the dishes because it was beyond the means of many people. What meat there is tends to be pork, lamb, and kid, with beef used more rarely and often being cooked for a long time because in the past the cheaper cuts were all that most people could afford. Chicken does appear in the regional cuisine, falling somewhere between the two categories. Today, the regional cuisine is still very much dominated by the precepts of *cucina povera*, with Campania's provinces, cities, towns, and islands all making their own contributions with key produce and signature dishes – lemons, walnuts, and dairy products from the Sorrento Peninsula; more lemons from Procida; the beloved San Marzano tomato of the Amalfi Coast; mussels, bluefish, and Annurca apples from the Phlegraean Fields; rabbit from Ischia; *mozzarella di bufala* and chestnuts from Caserta; apricots and cherry tomatoes from Vesuvius; anchovies, artichokes, and figs from Cilento; truffles and mushrooms from Irpinia; hazelnuts and walnuts from Benevento. The provinces of Benevento and Caserta give us their hearty peasant cuisine – as well as *torrone*, *nocino* (walnut liqueur), and Strega – while the island of Capri brings us limoncello and *insalata caprese* (see pages 112–13). In Naples, specialties include spaghetti with clams and, of course, pizza marinara and pizza Margherita. This list is by no means comprehensive, nor is the produce necessarily confined to the places named; it serves only to

illustrate the wealth and variety of what is so abundantly available in Naples and its surrounding districts and islands.

The region's food is also greatly influenced by the kitchens of the convents and monasteries of the Catholic Church. Not only did these institutions often cultivate great market gardens and sell their produce, but the Church's policy of providing food and shelter also meant that many great dishes have emerged from the convent/monastery tradition. One such example is the pastry *sfogliatelle* (see pages 146–7), now a popular Neapolitan speciality and sold in bakeries and *pasticcerie* all over the city, but which was originally concocted in the Croce della Lucca monastery, where it was made for visiting prelates.

And there is yet another layer to the cuisine of Naples and Campania, one provided by the royal and noble households of the past, under the rule of the Kingdoms of Sicily and Naples, the Spanish viceroys, and the later Bourbon court. The first had the effect of bringing spices into the kitchens of Naples, through alliances and trading with the Arabs (Naples was at this time a great port, with links to Genoa and the major trading routes of the time), while the Spanish were in power at a time when they and the Portuguese were bringing back new and strange fruits and vegetables from the New World – hence the arrival in the Neapolitan (and Campanian) diet of what are now staples such as tomatoes, chilies, potatoes, and beans. Under the French, chefs of the Bourbon court were brought from France and made their own influence felt in the form of rich sauces and ragùs, and what has now become the quintessentially Neapolitan *babà* (see pages 150–1). The more you look at the regional cuisine, the more complexities and interweavings you discover – all bound by the people's zest for life and their open hospitality.

AN ANCIENT WINE TRADITION

Campania has more to offer than a cuisine which excels in combining tastes and adding layers of tempting flavors. The region also has a long and fascinating history of viticulture. Legend has it that God wept when he recognized the Bay of Naples as a limb of the sky torn off by Lucifer. Where His celestial tears touched the ground, the so-called Lacryma Christi (Tears of Christ) grapevine sprung. Between myth and legend, viticulture in Campania dates back more than 3,000 years, to the time of Etruscan settlement. The region is, in fact, scattered with

archaeological remains and other evidence that testify to the long presence of grapevines and to the excellent quality of wine production. Wine was exported from Ischia during Roman times, for instance, and mention of Campanian wine is made by Horace.

Today, Campania produces on average around 52 million gallons of wine per year, of which 3.5 million gallons are certified DOC (Denominazione di Origine Controllata) and DOCG (Denominazione di Origine Controllata e Garantita). The former certification relates to the origin and production of the wine, the latter does the same, but with an official guarantee of origin.

Specifically, there are three types of DOCG wine: Taurasi, Fiano di Avellino, and Greco di Tufo. There are, on the other hand, 17 DOC wines: Aglianico del Taburno, Asprinio d'Aversa, Campi Flegrei, Capri, Castel San Lorenzo, Cilento, Costa d'Amalfi, Falerno del Massico, Galluccio, Guardiolo, Ischia, Penisola Sorrentina, Sannio, Sant'Agata dei Goti, Solopaca, Taburno, and Vesuvio. In addition, nine types of wine, both reds and whites, have a certification of regional distinctiveness (IGT, or Indicazione Geografica Tipica): Beneventano, Colli di Salerno, Dugenta, Epomeo, Irpinia, Paestum, Pompeiano, Roccamonfina, and Terre del Volturno. (For more on regional winemaking, see pages 72–3.)

Fortunately both for Campania and for wine lovers, viticulture and wine-making have undergone something of a transformation in the past few years, with standards and production techniques improving, new vineyards being planted, and renewed energy and commitment being seen throughout the industry.

SORRENTO CHEESES

This renewed energy is found across other agricultural sectors as well, lifting the economy and rejuvenating interest in products that have long been produced in the region, such as particularly fine mono-cultivar olive oils (see pages 20–1) and *mozzarella di bufala* (pages 44–5), to name just two. While *mozzarella di bufala* (buffalo mozzarella) is undoubtedly the most well known of Campania's distinctive regional cheeses, it is by no means the only variety that has its roots in this region.

The Sorrento Peninsula is an area with an ancient dairy tradition. At the beginning of the last century, Sorrento dairies supplied Naples with their products twice a week. The dairy products were placed on mallow leaves and shipped by rowboat across the Bay of Naples to the capital. That level of industriousness is still in evidence today, and towns such as Agerola on the Sorrento Peninsula are renowned for their quality cheeses, and especially for *fior di latte* (literally the "flower of the milk" and made from cow's milk), *caciocavallo*, ricotta, and *provola*. *Fior di latte* is made in the same fashion as *mozzarella di bufala*, with the same separation of curds, which are then stretched into shape by hand. The making of *fior di latte* is another of Campania's ancient traditions and has official PDO (protected designation of origin) status. The most famous *fior di latte* is produced in Agerola, a town whose origins date to pre-Roman times. During the time of the Greek physician Galen in the second century AD, Agerola was already renowned for the production of "very healthy milk." Top-quality cow's milk has always

been used for the production of *fior di latte*. This cheese is thus an integral part of the dairy heritage of Campania. It is spherical in shape and sometimes slightly flattened, with a white color that is less chalky than *mozzarella di bufala*, from which it can also be distinguished by its firmer texture and more delicate flavor.

Another important local cheese, *treccia sorrentina*, can in turn be distinguished from *fior di latte* by its distinctive shape and even firmer texture. Some dairies fold the extremities of the cheese, creating a shape that is reminiscent of a *tortano* (a type of Easter bread): this product is dubbed *tortaniello* locally. *Provola*, or provolone cheese, also has a spherical shape, is more or less flattened, and has a firmer texture than *fior di latte*, more like *treccia*. Its outer rind is whitish or ochre in color, which is not uniform when smoked (*provola affumicata*).

THE TOMATO – HALF STAPLE, HALF RELIGION

You cannot help but notice how many recipes from Naples and Campania involve the tomato. This fruit is so beloved in the region that people have been known to say that it is almost a religion. The *pomo amoris*, or *pomo d'oro* (literally, "golden apple"), may be of Peruvian origin, but it speaks the Campanian dialect perfectly, thriving and prospering in the climate, and fitting seamlessly into the region's traditions and cuisine. This is particularly true of the San Marzano plum tomato, grown mainly in the Agro Nocerino-Sarnese, which lies in the Sarno River valley between Naples and Salerno, and the Lattari and Picentini mountains, stretching down from the slopes of Vesuvius. This means a happy marriage between volcanic soil and a good water supply, providing perfect conditions for growing crops.

For more than two centuries after its arrival in Europe, the tomato was considered an ornamental plant, and only in the eighteenth century did it become widely and popularly accepted in cooking. Under Bourbon rule, the tomato became revered as an anointed prince of

cuisine. In Naples, it became a source of nourishment suitable for kings and farmers alike, until it reached its present celebrity status in the typical Mediterranean diet.

Campania was one of the first areas in Italy to cultivate and process the tomato, which is characteristically dubbed "red gold" and is spread throughout virtually every corner of the region. The San Marzano is, however, mostly grown in the fertile soil of the Agro Nocerino-Sarnese. This particular variety of tomato is known and valued all over the world for its flavor and texture, which are enhanced when it is processed into canned peeled tomatoes. It has a typically sweet but tart flavor, an elongated shape, and a flesh with few seeds or fibers. When fully ripe, this pulpy tomato is bright red in color and has a skin that is easily peeled off. Rich in flavor and nutritional value, it contains lycopene, beta-carotene, vitamin C, potassium, and sodium, as well possessing antioxidant properties.

Today, thanks to the fact that San Marzano tomatoes have been granted PDO status by the European Union, Campania can be justly proud of the unique flavor of this fruit, which is such an integral and defining element of its traditional dishes. There is a very strong bond between the San Marzano tomato and its land of origin. The people of Campania, with its volcanic soil and sunny temperate Mediterranean climate, prize the San Marzano not only as their very own variety of tomato, but also because of its now widespread commercial cultivation. On the small independent farms with their small lots of land scattered across the landscape, nature and tradition have given rise to an unbeatable combination of climate, sea, and history.

PASTA

When talking about the sun and heaven-blessed combinations, it would be difficult not to mention the pivotal role of pasta. It was during the nineteenth century that the making and eating of pasta became widespread in Campania, as demonstrated by the several pasta makers who began their activity at Torre Annunziata, Torre del Greco and Nola. The latter used to produce more than 200 kinds of "short" and "long" pasta. Whatever the much debated origins of pasta may be, it has an undeniably Neapolitan character, both as the main ingredient in the

Mediterranean diet and as a cultural expression. Pasta is, in fact, an element recurrently found in Neapolitan art and literature, and today the majority of the 180 Italian pasta companies are based in Campania.

Pasta is made of two basic and extremely simple ingredients: durum wheat flour and water. The first stage in the processing of the dough is called *granolatura* (kneading) and gives homogeneity to the product. Subsequently the dough is shaped through a process known as *trafilatura* (molding). This is still done by hand, using bronze *trafilati* (wirework molds) to obtain the pasta shape desired.

A fundamental part of the whole process is the drying stage, which is meticulously monitored. In Campania's pasta factories, drying is carried out at a temperature of 100°F and lasts between 24 and 36 hours, whereas this is done much faster in large-scale industrial production. According to a Campanian tradition, a good pasta has to "stand" during the cooking process. In other words, it must contain a sufficiently high level of gluten, the protein which keeps the flour together and prevents the pasta from disintegrating while cooking. These characteristics are enhanced by the slower methods used by Neapolitan pasta makers.

EXEMPLARY FRUITS

Campania is renowned for the cultivation of fruit, including apricots, apples, and lemons of very high quality. Lemon trees, first introduced by the Arabs, cling almost miraculously to the terraced fields that characterize the Neapolitan and Amalfi coast. One of the reasons why lemons grow so well and with such a wonderful flavor is the technique of using *pagliarelle* (straw mats), which are put over the foliage of the trees and supported by wooden posts in order to protect the plant from the cold and coastal winds – an ancient technique necessary during the coldest months of the year.

The Sorrento Peninsula and the island of Procida, in particular, yield lemons of a superior quality that are renowned all over the world for their taste and aroma. The skin, rich in essential oils, is used to flavor creams and ice creams, and to enhance the taste of traditional regional dishes. These are also the lemons, along with those grown on Capri, that are used to make the famous *limoncello* liqueur.

Olive oil, tomatoes, mozzarella, pasta, wines and spirits: all of these ingredients and more are combined in Neapolitan cuisine to create a perfect harmony of flavors, representing a synthesis of tradition, culture, and land. The bountiful region of Campania produces a cuisine that honors simple ingredients, satisfies the appetite, and soothes the soul with its lighthearted use of the best that nature has to offer.

ANTIPASTI,
ZUPPE E
MINESTRE

Appetizers and soups

COZZE AL PEPE
Peppered mussels

The simplicity of this typical fishermen's dish from the Borgo Marinari area of Naples belies the delicious results. The village of Borgo Marinari, just outside the fortress walls of the Castel dell'Ovo in Santa Lucia, Naples' ancient fishing quarter, was long home to fishermen who drew their daily catch from the Bay of Naples. A steaming bowl of these mussels will prove irresistible to any seafood lover.

✣ SERVES 4

2¹/₄ lb fresh mussels
plenty of freshly ground black pepper
lemon wedges, to serve

Rinse the mussels in plenty of cold water to remove any sand or grit, then scrub and remove the beards. Tap each mussel on the work surface and discard any that do not close or that have broken shells. Put the mussels in a large heavy saucepan, cover the pan, and cook over high heat for a few minutes until the shells open. Alternatively, cook the mussels on a hot grill or griddle pan.

When all the shells are open fully (discard any mussels that do not open), add lots of black pepper and stir for a minute or so. (Be careful not to overcook – otherwise the mussels will be rubbery.) Serve immediately with lemon wedges and some fresh, crusty bread.

CALAMARI E GAMBERONI AL PROFUMO DI MARE

Pan-fried squid and jumbo shrimp

Profumo di mare means "perfume of the sea," and evokes the essence of this dish, which originated in the convents of Campania, born out of the Church's long tradition of providing food and shelter in these institutions. As with all Neapolitan recipes, choose the freshest and best-quality ingredients that you can find. The entire region of Campania is renowned for the quality of its produce, and this is reflected in the approach to food and cooking in general.

✧ SERVES 4

3 tablespoons olive oil

1 garlic clove, finely chopped

1³/4 lb fresh squid, cleaned and cut into rings (see note)

12 cherry tomatoes, halved

8–12 fresh raw jumbo shrimp, unpeeled

7 oz mixed fresh shellfish such as mussels and clams, scrubbed and cleaned (see page 42)

salt and freshly ground black pepper

generous handful of fresh flat-leaf parsley, leaves picked and chopped, to garnish

Heat the oil in a large heavy frying pan over medium heat. Sweat the garlic for 2–3 minutes until soft and translucent. Add the squid and sweat for a few more minutes, being careful not to scorch the garlic. Add the cherry tomatoes and cook for 15 minutes, until the tomatoes break down and soften. Finally, add the unpeeled jumbo shrimp and the shellfish. Stir through, then continue cooking over medium heat for another 5 minutes, shaking the pan occasionally. Season with salt and black pepper, sprinkle with plenty of parsley, and serve immediately with slices of hot toasted bread such as crostini or ciabatta (rubbed with a cut piece of garlic and drizzled with a little extra virgin olive oil, then toasted).

Cleaning and preparing squid Clean and prepare the fresh squid by pulling the tentacles away from the body and removing the quill inside. Discard. Rinse the squid under cold running water, including the tentacles, then trim away the excess membrane at either side of the body and peel away the skin. Remove the tentacles, ink sac, and beak. Slice into rings or squares. When cutting squares, if you score the flesh lightly with a knife in a crisscross pattern, taking care not to cut the flesh all the way through, the squid will curl nicely when cooked.

MOZZARELLA IN CARROZZA
Mozzarella in a carriage

The name of this traditional Neapolitan speciality sums up these fantastic little sandwiches – the bread that forms the "carriage" encases meltingly hot mozzarella in a crisp shell for transportation to your mouth. Ideal as a snack as well as an appetizer, they make the most of their simple ingredients and will not last long on the plate.

⁜ SERVES 4–6

24 slices day-old crusty white bread
  such as ciabatta
12 slices buffalo mozzarella or
  fior di latte cheese, about
  $1/2$-in thick each
3 eggs
about $1/3$ cup milk
light olive oil for shallow-frying
salt and freshly ground black pepper
all-purpose flour for coating

Cut the bread to roughly the same size as the mozzarella slices, allowing a little extra around the edges for the cheese to spread. Sandwich each slice of mozzarella between 2 slices of bread, pressing down lightly around the edges of each one to "seal." Whisk the eggs with the milk until fluffy, and season with salt and black pepper.

Heat enough oil for shallow-frying (depending on the thickness of your sandwiches) in a heavy frying pan over medium heat. Lightly coat each of the little sandwiches in flour, then dip in the beaten egg, allowing the bread to soak up the eggy mixture. Carefully lower the sandwiches into the very hot oil, cooking a few at a time. Be careful not to crowd the pan, as the temperature of the oil will drop and your sandwiches will end up soggy, rather than crispy and light. Allow to cook for a few minutes until the cheese starts to melt and the bread is crisp and golden underneath. Using a spatula, turn the sandwiches over and press down Lightly flatten with the spatula. Cook for another 2–3 minutes, then remove and drain on paper towels.

These sandwiches are best piping hot and fresh from the pan, so serve immediately – with a warning about the hot melted cheese inside.

Variations If you like, make a paste out of 3 or 4 large anchovy filets packed in oil, and spread evenly over one side of the sandwiches before topping with the mozzarella. Alternatively, add the finely chopped leaves of a few sprigs of fresh oregano or thyme to the egg mixture used to coat the bread.

CARCIOFI CON MOZZARELLA
Baked artichokes stuffed with mozzarella

It is best to choose young, tender artichokes for this simple Neapolitan recipe. Look for the small purple-tinged ones, which have barely any choke at all, in spring and early summer – although obviously you need to make sure you pick ones large enough to stuff. If you cannot find baby artichokes, choose the most tender, juicy ones available. (The larger the artichokes, the tougher they will be.) The juices will keep the artichokes moist as they bake, and the leaves will be deliciously soft, pulling off easily as you eat them with their melting mozzarella stuffing.

✣ SERVES 4

12 young, tender globe artichokes or
   8 medium artichokes (depending on
   the season)
juice of 1 lemon
6 small balls of buffalo mozzarella
   cheese, about 5 oz in total, chopped
4 tablespoons freshly grated
   Parmesan cheese
4 tablespoons good-quality dried
   breadcrumbs (see note)
2 eggs, beaten
1 tablespoon olive oil plus extra for
   drizzling
salt and freshly ground black pepper

Preheat the oven to 350°F (180°C). Cut off the artichoke stems – you need to trim them so that you can stand the artichokes in the baking dish for cooking. Next trim about 1 inch off the tops of the artichokes, then snap off any tough outer leaves (if necessary, trim the tops of the larger leaves using a pair of scissors). Leave to soak for 30 minutes in a glass or ceramic bowl of cold water with the lemon juice added – make sure that the artichokes are covered to prevent discoloration. Drain, then scrape out and discard the fuzzy choke using a teaspoon and pull out any prickly inner leaves – the younger the artichokes, the less choke you will have to deal with. If you are using larger artichokes with very tightly packed leaves, you may need to blanch them in boiling water for a few minutes to soften slightly and loosen the leaves. Drain and set aside while you make the filling.

Put the mozzarella, Parmesan, breadcrumbs, eggs, and 1 tablespoon olive oil in a bowl. Season well with salt and black pepper. Mix the ingredients together well with a fork, and use the filling to stuff the artichokes. Using a spoon, push down the stuffing between the leaves as well as generously filling the center of each artichoke. Stand the artichokes in a single layer in an oiled baking dish or baking tray with shallow sides, add a little water, and drizzle with a little extra oil.

Bake in the preheated oven for about 45 minutes until tender, basting the artichokes frequently with any juices in the pan. Keep an eye on them and be careful not to overcook them; otherwise they will dry out. (Smaller artichokes will need less cooking time.) Serve immediately, while still piping hot.

Note It is easy to make your own dried breadcrumbs. Simply use up any leftover good-quality stale bread such as ciabatta or sourdough. Blend into medium-coarse breadcrumbs in a food processor, chop up with a knife, or break up with your hands. Spread the breadcrumbs on a flat baking sheet and leave in the oven at a very low heat until they are dried and toasty. (The ideal time to make them is after you have used the oven for something else – you can then utilize any residual heat to dry out the bread.) Use immediately or store in an airtight jar until needed. They should keep for up to 2 weeks.

OLIVE OIL

Like wine, extra virgin olive oil has been blessed with something of a renaissance in Campania, especially in relation to mono-cultivar olive oils (oil pressed from a single cultivar of olive tree from a single estate) and organically produced oils.

Olive oil was introduced to Campania by the Romans, who subsidized its production. Olive groves and estates, and hence olive oil production, spread virtally over the whole region but with a particular concentration in the Cilento area and on the Sorrento Peninsula. The Campanian tradition of making olive oil is among the most advanced to be found in the Mediterranean basin, where most of the world's olive production is based. The European Union has given Protected Designation of Origin (PDO) to two types of extra virgin olive oil produced in the Campania region, Olio Extra Vergine d'Oliva del Cilento and Olio Extra Vergine d'Oliva della Penisola Sorrentina, in order to safeguard their indisputable high quality.

These olive oils are highly prized, obtained from the first pressing of the fruits and produced from olive tree species native to Campania that have been cultivated since ancient times. They are rich in vitamins A, D, and E, and are characterized by low acidity and the presence of unsaturated fats. The benefits of olive oil in helping to prevent and control high levels of cholesterol are now widely known. Yet there was a time when the Neapolitan diet was considered very unhealthy because of the widespread use of this oil. How times change.

There are approximately 700 olive oil producers based in Campania. In a highly competitive global market, the quality and integrity of the product are key factors for success. With excellent raw materials at their disposal, small- and medium-sized olive oil producers in Campania have created a great product by monitoring quality at every stage of production and by adhering to the long-standing regional traditions that govern the making of olive oil in the region. Rather than being left behind by an increasingly mechanized agricultural world driven primarily by economic considerations, they have turned their artisan-like approach to the making of this traditional product very much to their advantage. Campanian extra virgin olive oil is becoming an increasingly competitive product on both domestic and foreign markets, drawing staunch devotees because of its high quality and flavor.

GNOCCHETTI E COZZE IN BRODETTO
Gnocchetti sardi and mussel soup

Gnocchetti sardi, slightly smaller than ordinary dried gnocchi, are also made with semolina flour. In this typical soup from Naples' Chiaia neighborhood, it is paired with fresh mussels to make a robust dish with clean flavors. Chiaia's origins lie in the 17th and 18th centuries with the Spanish, but today it plays host to high-end boutiques and Naples' hottest nightclubs.

✣ SERVES 4

3¼ lb fresh mussels
2 tablespoons olive oil
1 garlic clove, finely chopped
1 fresh red chili pepper, seeded and
   finely chopped
9 oz ripe cherry tomatoes, chopped
9 oz gnocchetti sardi or similar-
   shaped dried pasta such as
   orechiette
salt and freshly ground black pepper
handful of fresh flat-leaf parsley,
   leaves picked and chopped

Rinse the mussels in plenty of cold water to remove any grit, then scrub and remove the beards. Tap each mussel on the work surface and discard any that do not close or that have broken shells. Heat the oil in a pan over medium heat and sauté the garlic and chili for a few minutes until soft and starting to color. Remove the garlic and chili using a slotted spoon; discard.

Add the tomatoes to the garlic/chili-infused oil in the pan, and cook for about 10 minutes. Add the mussels, cover, and cook over medium-high heat until they open, shaking the pan frequently and stirring with a wooden spoon. When all the mussels have opened (discard any that remain closed), remove the pan from the heat. Leave to cool slightly, remove the shells, and return the mussel flesh to the tomato sauce.

In the meantime, cook the gnocchetti for half the recommended cooking time in a large pan of slightly salted boiling water. Drain and add to the mussels with a little of the cooking liquid – the soup should be a little liquidy, but not too watery. Return the pan to medium heat, season the soup with salt and black pepper, and cook for a few minutes. Sprinkle with chopped parsley and serve hot, with lots of freshly toasted bread to mop up the juices.

MINESTRA DI SCAROLE E FAGIOLI
White bean and escarole soup

Minestre are made with vegetables and meat, and are medium-thick like a broth or thick like the more well known minestrone, which usually contains pasta or rice. Very much from the *cucina povera* tradition, *minestre* have all the gusto of lots of traditional Italian soups and make a meal in themselves. They are often served topped with a grating of Parmesan cheese.

✣ SERVES 4

1 lb 2 oz dried cannellini beans
pinch of baking soda
1 garlic clove, peeled but left whole,
    plus 1 extra, finely chopped
1 celery stick
4 bunches of escarole, roughly
    chopped
3½ oz pancetta or bacon, diced
2 tablespoons olive oil
salt and freshly ground black pepper

Soak the beans overnight in plenty of cold water with a pinch of baking soda. Rinse well and put in a large heavy saucepan. Cover with 6 cups water and bring to a boil (do not add salt, as this toughens the skins). Add the whole garlic clove and the celery, cover the pan, and simmer over low heat for about 50 minutes or until the beans are cooked, but still with a slight bite, skimming off any froth that rises to the surface.

Just before the end of the cooking time, blanch the escarole in salted boiling water until just wilted. Drain well. Meanwhile, heat the oil in a deep-sided heavy frying pan over medium heat. Add the escarole, pancetta or bacon, and extra chopped garlic. Sweat for about 5 minutes until the pancetta is cooked and the garlic has softened. Remove the whole garlic and celery from the beans; discard. Add the beans with a little of their cooking liquid – just enough to make a medium-thick soup – to the pan. Season with salt and black pepper. Simmer gently for another 15 minutes. Serve hot.

ZUPPA DI FAGIOLI
Cannellini bean soup

The combination of cannellini beans and basil may seem like a slightly unusual one, but it gives this traditional bean soup from the Campanian countryside a deliciously fresh flavor.

✣ SERVES 4

1 lb 5 oz shelled fresh cannellini beans
⅓ cup olive oil
2 celery sticks, roughly chopped
3 garlic cloves
2 or 3 large fresh basil leaves
2 or 3 teaspoon fresh flat-leaf parsley,
    leaves picked and finely chopped
salt and freshly ground black pepper
freshly made croutons, to serve

Put the beans in a pot (preferably clay) with 7 cups cold water, cover, and bring to a boil. Reduce the heat to low and cook very gently for 2 hours. Just before the end of the cooking time, heat the oil in a pan over medium heat. Add the celery, garlic, and basil. Cover and leave to sweat for about 5 minutes until soft. Add to the beans with just enough water to make a thick soup. Season with salt and black pepper. Serve hot, with croutons scattered over the top of each serving.

Fresh cannellini beans Unless you are lucky enough to live in the hills of Benevento and Avellino, where premium cannellini beans are grown, you may find fresh cannellini beans difficult to find. If so, substitute with dried ones, soaking and rinsing as usual before cooking.

ZUPPA DI FAGIOLI E SCAROLA
Bread soup with cannellini beans and escarole

A traditional dish from the countryside surrounding Naples, this hearty and warming soup contains cannellini beans and toasted bread to satisfy the appetite, while the tomatoes add a lightness and zest that stop it from being too heavy. Escarole is best for the soup, as it has a milder flavor than its more bitter relatives, Belgian and curly endive. The secret is to blanch it slightly before adding to the soup, so that it retains its bright green color.

✣ SERVES 4

14 oz dried cannellini beans
pinch of baking soda
2 garlic cloves, finely chopped
1 celery stick, chopped
4¹/₂ oz crushed tomatoes
2 tablespoons olive oil
1 lb 6 oz escarole, leaves separated
  and roughly chopped
8 thick slices of freshly toasted
  day-old Italian bread such as
  ciabatta or pane casereccio
generous handful of fresh flat-leaf
  parsley, leaves picked and chopped
salt and freshly ground black pepper

Soak the beans overnight in plenty of cold water with a pinch of baking soda. Rinse well and transfer to a large heavy saucepan. Cover well with plenty of cold fresh water (about 5 cups). Add the garlic, celery, tomatoes, and oil. Season with salt and black pepper. Bring to a boil, then reduce the heat and simmer for about 50 minutes or until the beans still have a slight bite to them, rather than being mushy. Skim off any froth that rises to the surface as the beans cook.

Just before the beans are cooked, blanch the escarole in a separate saucepan of salted boiling water for a few minutes until it has just wilted. Drain and add to the beans. Check and adjust the seasoning if necessary. To serve, lay 2 slices of the toasted bread in the bottom of each of the serving bowls, ladle the soup, sprinkle with the parsley, and serve immediately.

ZUPPA DI FAVE SECCHE
Stewed fava beans

More of a side dish than a soup, this recipe originates from the region around Mount Vesuvius and makes a hearty winter dish. Dried fava beans are used here, but you can make a version with fresh fava beans when they are in season. Simply blanch in boiling water for a couple of minutes if necessary to loosen the skins, then slip the pods out of their skins before adding to the pan (you will also need a much shorter cooking time). Slow, gentle cooking, however, is still important – a fundamental part of most Campanian regional cuisine.

✣ SERVES 4

1 lb 2 oz dried fava beans
pinch of baking soda
$3^{1}/_{2}$ oz pancetta or bacon, diced
1 garlic clove, finely chopped
2 onions, finely chopped
4 cups hot water
about 2 tablespoons good-quality
  extra virgin olive oil
generous handful of fresh flat-leaf
  parsley, leaves picked and chopped
salt and freshly ground black pepper

Soak the beans in cold water overnight with a pinch of baking soda. Melt the pancetta or bacon in a large pan over medium heat, and sweat the garlic and onions, but do not allow to brown. When the onions are soft and start to caramelize, add half of the hot water and bring to a boil. Add the fava beans and cover with the remaining hot water. Return to a boil and continue cooking at this temperature for 10 minutes.

Reduce the heat to low, skim off any froth from the surface and season with salt and black pepper. Cook, covered, over very gentle heat for about 4 hours until the beans are barely tender, taking care that they do not stick to the bottom of the pan. Check the seasoning, then transfer to a serving dish. Serve hot, drizzled with the olive oil and sprinkled with plenty of chopped parsley.

ZUPPA DI PATATE E CARCIOFI
Potato and artichoke soup

Potatoes and artichokes make a good pairing, and the slow cooking in this classic Neapolitan recipe ensures that their textures meld together for a harmonious balance and satisfying flavor.

✣ SERVES 4

$2^{1}/_{4}$ lb starchy potatoes, such as
  Russet
6 fresh artichokes
1 onion, finely chopped
1 lb 2 oz fresh ripe tomatoes,
  preferably plum, chopped
2 tablespoons olive oil
2 teaspoons dried oregano
salt and freshly ground black pepper

Peel, rinse, and chop the potatoes into $^{1}/_{2}$ inch cubes. Rinse the artichokes, remove the tough outer leaves, and cut into slices. Using a knife or a spoon, scrape off and discard any choke or prickly inner leaves. Put the potatoes and artichokes into a large heavy saucepan and add the onion, tomatoes, oil, and oregano. Cover with twice the depth of water, so that if your vegetables are 1 inch deep, for instance, the water comes up to a depth of 2 inches. Season with salt and black pepper, and cook over gentle heat for about an hour. Serve hot.

PASTA E RISO

Pasta and rice

MACCHERONCELLI ARRABBIATI
Maccheroncelli with tomato and chili

Perhaps one of the best-known of the *cucina povera* pasta sauces, *arrabbiati* is traditionally made with *ciccioli,* or pork scratchings – no part of a beast is wasted and cheap cuts are always used to their best advantage. Two other fundamental ingredients in this spicy sauce are tomatoes and chili; it is the latter that gives the sauce its name – *arrabbiato* means "angry" in Italian.

✛ SERVES 4

1 lb 2 oz maccheroncelli, such as
  bucatini or ziti, broken up into
  pieces, or shorter dried tubular pasta
  such as penne rigate
2 oz lard or olive oil
1 onion, finely chopped
3^1/$_2$ oz pancetta or bacon or ciccioli,
  diced
10 oz fresh ripe tomatoes, preferably
  plum, chopped
1 fresh red chili, seeded and
  finely chopped
freshly ground black pepper
freshly shaved or grated Parmesan
  cheese, to serve
freshly shaved or grated pecorino
  cheese, to serve

Bring a large pan of slightly salted water to a boil and cook the pasta until al dente.

    Meanwhile, melt the lard or heat the olive oil in a heavy frying pan over medium-high heat. Add the onion and sweat for a few minutes until soft, then add the pancetta, bacon, or ciccioli along with the tomatoes and chili. Season with black pepper. Cook for a few minutes, stirring all the time so the sauce does not stick. Drain the pasta, add to the sauce, and stir through. Sprinkle with lots of grated Parmesan and pecorino, and serve immediately.

BUCATINI CON I PEPERONCINI
Bucatini with green peperoncini, tomatoes, and basil

A classic *cucina povera* dish, this one features green *peperoncini*: small sweet peppers with a hint of heat that are sometimes known as Tuscan or sweet Italian peppers. They are often pickled and sold in jars as an antipasto or for use in salads or as a garnish.

✣ SERVES 4

2 tablespoons olive oil

1 lb 2 oz small green *peperoncini* (see note), seeded and chopped

2 garlic cloves, finely chopped

1 lb 2 oz canned peeled whole plum tomatoes, chopped

3 or 4 large fresh basil leaves, torn into small pieces

1 lb 2 oz bucatini (perciatelli) or similar long tubular pasta such as mezzanelli

Heat the oil in a frying pan over medium heat. Add the *peperoncini* and sweat for a few minutes until soft. As soon as they are cooked, remove from the frying pan with a slotted spoon and set aside. Using the same oil, sweat the garlic for a couple of minutes until soft. Add the tomatoes and basil. Bring to a simmer, then reduce the heat and cook gently for 30 minutes. Return the *peperoncini* to the pan and keep the sauce warm.

Meanwhile, cook the bucatini in a large pan of slightly salted boiling water until al dente. Drain and serve topped with the tasty sauce.

Note The *peperoncini* used here are mildly hot, curved, sweet red chilies. They are usually picked when they are 2–3 inches long. Mature red ones have slightly wrinkled skin and taper to a blunt lobed end; green *peperoncini* are the same variety picked before ripening. If you cannot find *peperoncini*, use another mild sweet pepper, or replace with sliced eggplant.

FUSILLI CON LA RICOTTA
Fusilli with ricotta, tomatoes, and Parmesan

One of the by-products of buffalo mozzarella is buffalo ricotta. It has a more intense flavor than cow's milk ricotta and beautifully combines with the acidity of the tomatoes to make a smooth, creamy sauce. Don't worry if you cannot find buffalo ricotta; ordinary ricotta will work just as well.

✣ SERVES 4

2 tablespoons olive oil

1 small onion, finely chopped

2 1/4 lb canned whole peeled plum tomatoes

14 oz fusilli

9 oz fresh ricotta cheese

1 tablespoon freshly grated Parmesan cheese, plus extra for serving

3 or 4 large fresh basil leaves, torn into small pieces

salt and freshly ground black pepper

Heat the oil in a pan over medium heat and sweat the onion gently until soft and starting to caramelize. Reduce to low heat, add the tomatoes, and simmer very gently for 1 hour, breaking them up with a wooden spoon as they cook down. The longer you simmer the sauce, the tastier the tomatoes will be.

Cook the fusilli in a large pan of slightly salted boiling water until al dente. While the pasta is cooking, mix the ricotta with a ladleful of the cooking water. Add a little tomato sauce and grated Parmesan, and mix to a smooth cream. Drain the pasta and add the ricotta mixture and the remaining tomato sauce. Season with salt and black pepper. Mix well, sprinkle over the basil and extra grated Parmesan, and serve.

SALSA GENOVESE
Beef, onion, and wine sauce

Despite the "salsa" in the name, this is a classic *ragù*. It is also very Neapolitan in origin, rather than from Genoa, as the second half of the title implies. Debates on the origin of its name abound, but what is not in question is its place in the culinary heritage of Naples and its origins in the 16th century. The balance of ingredients has altered over the years. When Naples was not so affluent, much less meat was used, and there has also been an increasing emphasis on onions. It is a dish that is often eaten on Sundays, and can be served in two parts, as different courses. For the first course, the meat is removed from the sauce and set aside, and freshly cooked al dente pasta is added to the gently simmering sauce and mixed through. This is then served topped with a drizzle of extra virgin olive oil and a sprinkling of freshly shaved Parmesan cheese. The second course is made up of the meat, dressed in a little of the sauce, which is served with vegetable side dishes. This version, however, uses minced beef, rather than a whole piece of meat that is later sliced, and works well on a bed of freshly cooked pasta.

❖ SERVES 4–6

3 tablespoons olive oil

2 tablespoons lard

1 lb 6 oz onions, sliced into rings

1 lb 2 oz lean ground beef

3 carrots, sliced

2 celery sticks, sliced

1 oz salami napoli, diced

1 oz prosciutto crudo or cured pork
  shoulder, diced

1/3 cup passata

1 cup dry white wine

salt and freshly ground black pepper

Heat the oil and lard in a large heavy saucepan over medium heat. Add the onions and sweat for a few minutes until soft, then add the beef, carrots, celery, salami, and prosciutto or cured pork shoulder. Cook, stirring and breaking up the beef with a wooden spoon, until the meat has browned. Dilute the passata with a little warm water and add to the pan. When the liquid has reduced completely, pour over the wine and leave the sauce to simmer gently, covered, for at least 2 hours.

Just before serving, mash down the sauce with a fork until the onions are smooth. Serve hot with al dente pasta such as rigatoni or paccheri.

PENNETTE PRIMAVERA
Pasta with spring vegetables

This is a quintessential springtime dish from the *cucina povera* tradition. Choose zucchinis with firm skins, making sure to avoid the larger ones, which are watery and filled with seeds. They are best when young and small.

✢ SERVES 4

10 oz zucchinis

a little olive oil

2 hard-boiled eggs, chopped

14 oz pennette such as penne rigate or similar

about 1³/₄ oz butter, cut into small pieces

freshly grated Parmesan cheese

salt and freshly ground black pepper

fresh mint leaves, to serve

Top and tail the zucchinis and halve lengthwise. Cut into strips. Heat a little olive oil in a pan over medium-high heat, and sauté the zucchinis for a few minutes until golden brown. Season with salt and black pepper, then transfer to a serving bowl with the chopped eggs.

Meanwhile, cook the pennette in a large saucepan of slightly salted boiling water until al dente. Drain and transfer with a little of the cooking water (just enough to keep the pasta moist) to the bowl with the zucchinis and eggs. Stir in a generous amount of butter and grated Parmesan, mixing thoroughly but gently, so that you do not break up the eggs too much. Garnish with the mint leaves and sprinkle with plenty of black pepper. Serve immediately.

SPAGHETTI AL FILETTO DI POMODORO
Spaghetti with tomatoes and basil

When you think of the classic tomato sauce for spaghetti, this is the recipe that should top your list. You can also use it as a base when a recipe calls for tomato sauce as one of the ingredients.

✢ SERVES 4

2 tablespoons olive oil

2 garlic cloves, finely chopped

14 oz canned peeled whole plum tomatoes, drained, seeded, and chopped, or 14 oz fresh plum tomatoes, peeled, seeded, and chopped (see page 116)

generous handful of fresh basil leaves, finely sliced

pinch of sugar

salt

14 oz spaghetti

Heat the oil in a pan over medium heat and sweat the garlic for a few minutes until soft and starting to caramelize. Add the tomatoes, half of the basil, and a pinch of sugar. Season with salt and simmer over gentle heat for at least 15 minutes.

Cook the spaghetti in a large pan of slightly salted boiling water until al dente. Drain and mix with the sauce. Sprinkle the remaining basil over the top and serve immediately.

Note When using canned tomatoes, always buy whole peeled plum tomaotes; they are more flavorful and better quality than those sold already chopped. Adding sugar to the sauce not only cuts the acidity of the tomato, but also helps to bring out its flavor. This works particularly well when you are using fresh tomatoes (as you can in this dish if you like).

PASTA E CECI
Pasta and chickpeas

Pasta mista and dried chickpeas combine in this warm, hearty dish that shows its country roots in its rustic nature and use of legumes. Simplicity is key, and this nourishing dish will banish the chill – and your hunger – on a cold winter's day.

✤ SERVES 4

9 oz dried chickpeas
pinch of baking soda
10 oz pasta mista or raganelle
2 tablespoons olive oil
1–2 garlic cloves, finely chopped
2 teaspoons chopped fresh
  oregano leaves
handful of fresh flat-leaf parsley,
  leaves picked and chopped
salt and freshly ground black pepper

Soak the chickpeas overnight in plenty of cold water with a pinch of baking soda. Rinse well and transfer to a heavy saucepan. Cover well with fresh water, and bring to a boil over medium heat. Do not add salt initially, as this toughen the skins. Reduce the heat and simmer for about 3 hours until the beans are tender but still have a slight bite. Season with the oil, garlic, oregano, salt, and black pepper, and keep on a gentle simmer.

Cook the pasta for half its cooking time in a large pan of slightly salted boiling water. Drain and add to the chickpeas. When the pasta is cooked al dente, transfer the pasta and chickpeas to a serving dish, sprinkle with the parsley, and serve immediately.

PASTA E LENTICCHIE
Pasta and lentils

Lentils are a good source of iron, and also contain important nutrients such as calcium and vitamins A and B. In Campania, particularly in the remote and mountainous rural areas where meat was not always available, beans and legumes became an important addition to the diet. They were used to make tasty, filling dishes that could be eaten over the winter months, as demonstrated in this simple dish from the region around Mount Vesuvius.

✤ SERVES 4

10 oz brown lentils, picked and rinsed
2 garlic cloves, crushed
2 tablespoons olive oil
3 canned whole peeled plum
  tomatoes
2 or 3 teaspoons fresh flat-leaf
  parsley leaves, chopped
14 oz tubetti
salt and freshly ground black pepper

Put the lentils into a saucepan and cover with plenty of cold water. Cover the pan with a lid and cook over low heat for 1½ hours until soft. Add the garlic, oil, tomatoes, and parsley, and season with salt and black pepper. Continue cooking for another 30 minutes.

Cook the pasta in a large pan of slightly salted boiling water for half its cooking time. Drain and add to the lentils, and continue cooking until the pasta is al dente. Let stand for 5 minutes before serving.

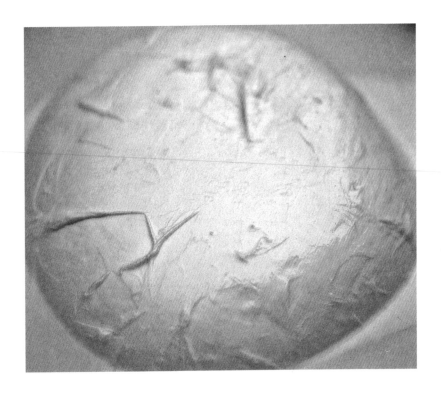

SPAGHETTI ALLA CAPRESE
Spaghetti with tuna, anchovies, tomatoes, and olives

The ingredients used in this spaghetti recipe are typical of those found in dishes cooked in family kitchens on the island of Capri. Tuna, anchovies, tomatoes, and olives crop up in different combinations in various other dishes from Campania. They may all have strong flavors, but they work well together to provide a wonderful gutsy taste explosion.

✤ SERVES 4

4 tablespoons olive oil
1 lb 2 oz canned whole peeled plum tomatoes
7-oz jar tuna in oil, drained
1³/₄ oz salted anchovy filets, chopped
1³/₄ oz Gaeta or similar black olives, pitted and halved
3¹/₂ oz buffalo mozzarella, finely diced
14 oz spaghetti
salt and freshly ground black pepper

Heat 2 tablespoons of the oil in a pan over medium heat and add the tomatoes. Simmer gently for 10 minutes until the sauce has thickened. Season with salt and black pepper.

In a separate pan, heat the remaining 2 tablespoons of oil over medium heat. Add the tuna and use a wooden spoon to break it up into flakes. Add the anchovies and olives, and stir through. Add the finely diced mozzarella to the thickened tomato sauce.

Cook the spaghetti in a large pan of slightly salted boiling water until al dente. Drain and mix with the tuna sauce. Transfer to a serving dish and add the tomato and mozzarella sauce. Stir gently and serve immediately.

SPAGHETTI ALLA ROSINELLA
Spaghetti with shrimp, squid, and clams

In this typical pasta dish from the Posillipo district of Naples, the most is made of the fresh seafood available along the coast of Campania. Posillipo, situated at the western end of the Bay of Naples and leading down to the water, is one of the oldest areas in the city – references to it can be found in both classical Greek and Roman works. Today, it is very much a residential quarter, but glimpses of its early history can be found in the Roman ruins at the water's edge. There are also remains of the villa complex of Roman equestrian and contemporary of Emperor Augustus, Vedius Pollius, including an amphitheater perched on the cliffs above the bay.

✣ SERVES 4

2 tablespoons olive oil
2 garlic cloves, finely chopped
1 fresh red chili, seeded and
  finely chopped
10 oz fresh clams, scrubbed and
  rinsed well (see note)
2 fresh squid, cleaned and prepared,
  cut into rings or small squares (see
  note on page 16)
7–8 oz fresh raw shrimp, peeled and
  deveined
14 oz spaghetti
salt and freshly ground black pepper
fresh flat-leaf parsley, chopped,
  to serve

Heat the oil in a large pan over medium heat and sweat the garlic and chili for a few minutes until soft. Tap the clams on the work surface and discard any that do not close. Add the clams and squid to the pan with half of the garlic and half of the chili, and continue to sweat, taking care that the garlic and chili do not burn. As soon as the clams open (discard any that do not), tip the contents of the pan onto a plate and set aside. Add the shrimp to the same pan with the remaining garlic and chili, and sauté over medium-high heat for a few minutes until cooked. Pick the flesh from the clam shells, discard the shells, and return the flesh to the pan with the squid, garlic, and chili. (If you prefer, you can keep the clams in their shells for serving.) Season with salt and a little black pepper, and toss to heat through.

Meanwhile, cook the spaghetti in a large pan of slightly salted boiling water until al dente. Drain and add to the sauce with a tiny amount of the cooking water (just enough to keep the pasta moist). Stir well, transfer to a large serving bowl or individual pasta bowls, and sprinkle with lots of chopped parsley. Serve immediately.

Preparing clams Tap the clams on the work surface and discard any that do not close. Scrub the clams well under cold running water to wash away any grit. If you are not using farmed clams, you may need to purge them of sand or grit, but a good scrub on the outside and proper rinsing should do the trick. Otherwise, put the clams in a large bowl of salted water, making sure they are well covered (but do not cover the bowl). Soak in the refrigerator for a couple of hours or even overnight – any grit or sand will be left behind in the bottom of the bowl when you remove the clams. Rinse in plenty of fresh cold water, then strain the water through a fine cloth such as muslin or a clean dishcloth. You then pick out your clams and discard the grit. (Or you could simply rinse under cold running water.)

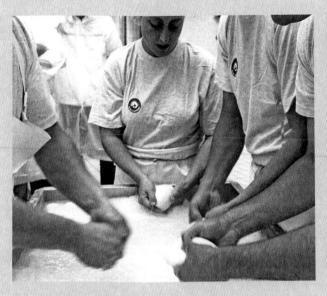

MOZZARELLA DI BUFALA

At Campania Felix, situated on the plains of the Caserta province between Francolise and Grazzanize, the family have been making *mozzarella di bufala*, or buffalo mozzarella, for more than 100 years. And it is more than simply a business to them – it's an operation that still very much reflects the ethos of founder Enrico Parente, who said in 1919. "Only buffalo milk, milk enzymes, rennet and salt. These are the only ingredients to produce my mozzarella. High-quality mozzarella! On my word of honor."

They can guarantee the quality of their product because they own the herd of buffalo, and the entire process from milking to finished cheese takes only 12 hours. The animals are milked at four in the morning. The milk is instantly pasteurized, then a natural fermenting agent is added to encourage it to curdle. Curds are separated from the whey, and the whey is made into ricotta. The remaining curd is salted, shredded, and cooled to make the mozzarella base. This is then placed in boiling water and stirred to melt it. Pieces are pulled off by hand either to make the familiar mozzarella balls or to be stretched into plaits. The balls and plaits are packed in slightly salted water to keep them fresh. The cheese is ready to be shipped at four in the afternoon.

The evident passion for making mozzarella – and its by-product ricotta, as well as other regional cheeses such as *caciocavallo* and *provola affumicata* – is far from restricted to the people at Campania Felix, or to the province of Caserta. *Mozzarella di bufala campana* is highly prized and considered the true gem of Campania. It is certainly distinctly the region's own, and is increasingly gaining recognition in a demanding European market, as well as an ever-growing global one.

Although *mozzarella di bufala campana* has been made for hundreds of years (the water buffalo was introduced to Italy more than a thousand years ago), it is only in the past century or so that this cheese has been made as a commercial product. Today, the production chain involved in making and selling *mozzarella di bufala* is crucially important to the agricultural and wider economy of the region, where more than 400 independent dairy companies operate. In recognition of this, Campania's buffalo mozzarella was granted PDO (Protected Designation of Origin) status in 1996, a mark of authenticity and quality.

Buffalo mozzarella should not be confused with *fior di latte*, which is made in a similar fashion but from cow's milk. Although delicious, it lacks buffalo mozzarella's characteristic tang and has a lower fat and protein content.

VERMICELLI CON SUGO DI POLIPI
Vermicelli with octopus sauce

Although some people think of octopus as being tough, this need not be the case. All it takes is a little care in the cooking – some octopus, some tomatoes, a little garlic, a little oil, and a little slow-cooking. Once again, the approach in this dish from the Borgo Marinari is very much about the Neapolitan attitude of treating your ingredients with respect.

✢ SERVES 4

1 lb 2 oz small octopus, rinsed

1 lb 2 oz ripe tomatoes,
  peeled and seeded

2 garlic cloves, crushed

about 2 tablespoons olive oil

1 lb 6 oz vermicelli

salt and freshly ground black pepper

chopped fresh flat-leaf parsley,
  to serve

Put the octopus, tomatoes, garlic, and oil in a terracotta or similar flameproof casserole dish. Season with salt and black pepper. Cover the dish with foil, then put on the lid (alternatively, you can use a pressure cooker). Cook over gentle heat for about 30 minutes until the sauce turns a very dark color.

Just before the sauce is ready, cook the vermicelli in a large pan of slightly salted boiling water until al dente. Drain and add to the sauce. Stir through, sprinkle generously with the parsley, and serve immediately.

Tip Do not worry if you cannot find fresh octopus where you live. Frozen octopus serves just as well and in many ways is as good as fresh because it is cleaned and frozen immediately, rather than facing a journey to the market or fish dealer.

FARFALLE CON TONNO E PISELLI
Farfalle with tuna and peas

The Sorrento peninsula is dotted with citrus groves and olive trees, and is a rich source of both produce and culinary inspiration – lemons, walnuts, pasta, cheese and dairy products, fish and seafood. The recipe here is typical of family recipes found along this enchanting coastline.

✢ SERVES 4

2 tablespoons olive oil

1 onion, finely chopped

12 oz shelled fresh or frozen
  green peas

7-oz jar tuna in oil, drained

14 oz farfalle

generous handful of fresh flat-leaf
  parsley, chopped

salt and freshly ground black pepper

Heat the oil in a pan over medium heat. Add the onion and sweat for a few minutes until soft and transparent. Add the peas and 1 cup water. Season with salt and black pepper. Cover and leave to simmer for about 15 minutes. Using a fork, break the tuna up into largish flakes and add to the peas. Continue cooking for a few more minutes.

Meanwhile, cook the pasta in a large pan of slightly salted boiling water until al dente. Drain, add to the sauce, and stir through. Sprinkle over the chopped parsley and serve immediately.

LINGUINE CON VONGOLE E POMODORI
Linguine with clams and tomatoes

Clams are highly prized along the Campanian coastline. This dish comes from Naples' Borgo Marinari area, the source of many recipes that take advantage of the region's harvest from the sea.

✣ SERVES 4

2¹/₄ lb clams, scrubbed and cleaned
  (see note on page 42)
2 tablespoons olive oil
1 garlic clove, finely chopped
1 lb 2 oz ripe tomatoes, peeled and
  seeded (see page 116)
a couple of small crabs (optional)
1 lb 5 oz linguine
handful of fresh flat-leaf parsley,
  leaves picked and chopped
salt and freshly ground black pepper

Put the clams in a heavy saucepan. Add a little water, cover the pan, and steam over medium-high heat until the shells open (discard any that do not). Remove the flesh and discard the shells. Heat the oil in a heavy frying pan over medium heat. Sauté the clam flesh and garlic for a few minutes until the garlic is soft and starting to color. Add the tomatoes and season with salt. Stir through and cook for another few minutes until the tomato starts to break down.

Pour the sauce into a flameproof clay pot or casserole, and simmer over medium heat for about 15 minutes. Crush the crabs, if using, with a mortar and pestle, and put in a tightly bound cloth bag or piece of muslin. Plunge into the sauce while it is cooking. Leave for a few minutes to release the flavor, then discard.

Cook the linguine in a large pan of slightly salted boiling water until al dente. Drain, add to the sauce, and stir through. Serve with a sprinkling of freshly ground black pepper and chopped parsley.

BUCATINI ALLA "SETTEMBRINI"
Tricolor pasta

The three colors in this pasta dish represent the colors of the Italian flag. Simple but filling, it makes the perfect dish to serve for a lunch with friends and family. It is easy to increase the quantities if you want to serve more people.

❖ SERVES 4–6

2¼ lb bucatini or similar dried pasta such as fettuccine or linguine
10 oz zucchinis, cut into julienne or slices
1 garlic clove, finely chopped (optional)
5 oz butter
1 quantity tomato sauce (see note at right and Spaghetti al filetto di pomodoro on page 37)
5 oz Parmesan cheese, grated
salt and freshly ground black pepper

Cook the pasta in a large pan of slightly salted water until al dente; drain, saving a little of the cooking liquid. Meanwhile, blanch the zucchinis in boiling water for 30 seconds; drain. Sauté the zucchinis and garlic, if using, in half the butter in a heavy frying pan over medium heat for a few minutes. Season with salt and black pepper. Melt the remaining butter.

Arrange the pasta on three serving dishes or in a three-section rectangular serving dish as follows. In the left-hand section, put one-third of the pasta mixed with a generous amount of hot tomato sauce – keep it warm on the stove until you need it. In the middle section, put another third mixed with the melted butter and lots of freshly grated Parmesan. In the right-hand section, put the last third of pasta mixed with the sautéed zucchinis.

Tomato sauce Homemade tomato sauce is far tastier than store-bought versions. Use the recipe on page 37 and, if you like, substitute the canned tomatoes with 1 lb 2 oz peeled, seeded, and chopped fresh plum tomatoes. Follow the method as given, but simmer gently for 30 minutes.

LINGUINE CON LA PANCETTA
Linguine with pancetta and tomato sauce

There is no avoiding the Neapolitans' passionate culinary relationship with the tomato and, as this traditional Easter dish clearly and deliciously shows, why would you want to?

❖ SERVES 4

2 tablespoons olive oil
1 onion, finely chopped
3½ oz pancetta, diced
2¼ lb ripe tomatoes, peeled and chopped (see note on page 116)
2 or 3 large fresh basil leaves, plus extra, finely sliced, to garnish
14 oz linguine
2 tablespoons freshly grated Parmesan cheese

Heat the oil in a pan over medium heat and sauté the onion and pancetta. Add the tomatoes and simmer over low heat for 20 minutes. Tear the whole basil leaves into small pieces, sprinkle into the sauce, and cook for another 10 minutes.

Cook the linguine in a large pan of slightly salted boiling water until al dente. Drain and add to the sauce. Stir through, then sprinkle the extra basil and Parmesan over the top. Serve immediately.

PENNETTE AL FORMAGGIO AL FORNO
Baked pennette with four cheeses

A *cucina povera* recipe, this pasta bake takes advantage of the array of cheeses produced in Campania, including the oddly named *caciocavallo* (horse's cheese).

✢ SERVES 4–6

1 lb 2 oz pennette such as
   penne rigate
3¹/₂ oz butter, plus extra for
   top of dish
5 oz thickly sliced cooked ham,
   preferably Italian, diced
3¹/₂ oz fontina cheese, diced
3¹/₂ oz caciocavallo cheese, diced
7 oz provola affumicata (smoked
   provolone cheese), diced
freshly grated Parmesan cheese
generous handful of coarse dried
   breadcrumbs (see note on page 19)
salt and freshly ground black pepper

Preheat the oven to 300°F (150°C). Cook the pennette in a large saucepan of slightly salted boiling water for 12 minutes until al dente.

While the pasta is cooking, melt the butter in a pan over medium heat and lightly brown the diced ham. Drain the pasta and add to the ham and butter. Add the fontina, caciocavallo, and provola, mix well and transfer to a buttered baking dish. Sprinkle generously with grated Parmesan and top with the breadcrumbs. Dot with some extra butter and bake for 15 minutes. Serve immediately while the cheese is nice and stringy.

Caciocavallo cheese Similar to aged provolone, *caciocavallo* is made out of sheep's or cow's milk, has a hard edible rind, and is shaped like a teardrop. The method for making it is believed to date from at least the fourteenth century and originated in Sicily. *Caciocavallo* literally means "horse's cheese," a name that seems to have come from the way the cheese is left to dry by hanging two curds attached by string so that they straddle a horizontal pole or beam – *a cavallo*. Caciocavallo Silano (PDO) is a cow's milk version of the cheese that is made in designated areas of Campania, as well as in Basilicata, Calabria, Molise, and Puglia.

LASAGNETTE CON LA RICOTTA
Fresh pasta bake with ricotta

Lasagnette is a narrower version of lasagne pasta. Like lasagne, its sheets can be wavy along one side or both, or straight along the edges. This pasta bake is often served during *Carnevale*, the traditional period of celebration before the advent of Lent.

✢ SERVES 4

7 oz fresh ricotta
1³/₄ oz butter, melted
1³/₄ oz Parmesan cheese, grated, plus
   extra for sprinkling
pinch of freshly ground nutmeg
1 lb 2 oz lasagnette
salt and freshly ground black pepper

Preheat the oven to 300°–325°F (150°–160°C). Mix the ricotta in a bowl with a little hot water, half of the melted butter, the Parmesan, and a pinch of nutmeg. Season with salt and pepper. Set aside.

Cook the lasagnette in a large saucepan of slightly salted boiling water until al dente. Drain, then arrange a third of the pasta in a layer over the bottom of a large buttered ovenproof dish. Cover with a layer of the ricotta cream. Repeat the process, finishing off with a layer of pasta. Sprinkle with some extra grated Parmesan, pour over the remaining melted butter, and bake in the oven for about 30 minutes until the top is crispy and golden brown. Cut into slices and serve hot.

MACCHERONCELLI CON LE MELANZANE
Maccheroncelli with eggplant and cherry tomatoes

Cherry tomatoes and eggplants – and other vegetables and fruit – thrive in the region of rich volcanic soil around Mount Vesuvius, from where this recipes comes. They are used here to make a sauce for *maccheroncelli*, a long tube-shaped pasta slightly less thick than a pencil.

✣ SERVES 4

2 1/4 lb eggplants
light olive oil for shallow-frying
1 lb 5 oz maccheroncelli or similar
  long tube-shaped pasta such
  as bucatini or perciatelli
10 oz cherry tomatoes, halved
about 2 tablespoons extra virgin olive
  oil for seasoning
1 tablespoon grated pecorino cheese
salt

Slice the eggplants and sprinkle with salt. Put in a colander and place a weight on top. Leave the eggplants to drain for 1 hour to draw out any bitter juices and the excess water. Rinse well under cold running water, shake the water off and pat the eggplants dry with a clean cloth or paper towels.

Heat enough oil for shallow-frying in a heavy pan over medium-high heat. Shallow-fry the eggplants on both sides until crispy. Remove with a slotted spoon and drain on paper towels.

In the meantime, cook the pasta in a large pan of slightly salted boiling water until al dente. Drain. Add the eggplants, cherry tomatoes, and extra virgin olive oil. Stir well, sprinkle with the pecorino, and serve immediately.

PASTA E FAGIOLI
Pasta with cannellini beans

This is very much a country dish. In areas where meat was scarce or expensive, legumes were often used to provide necessary protein in the diet – with the added benefit that they were filling and could be used over the winter months when fresh produce was less available.

✣ SERVES 4

10 oz dried cannellini beans
pinch of baking soda
2 tablespoons olive oil
2 garlic cloves, finely chopped
2 celery sticks, chopped
2 fresh tomatoes, peeled, seeded, and
  chopped (see page 116)
1 fresh red chili, seeded and
  finely chopped
2 tablespoons passata
10 oz pasta mista
salt and freshly ground black pepper

Soak the beans overnight in plenty of cold water with a pinch of baking soda. Rinse well, and put the beans in a pan with 6 cups water. Cover the pan and bring to a boil. Reduce the heat to low and simmer gently for 2 hours until the beans are tender but still have a bite.

In the meantime, make a tomato sauce. Heat the oil in a frying pan over medium heat. Add the garlic, celery, tomatoes, and chili. Reduce the heat and simmer gently for 10 minutes until cooked down into a sauce.

When the beans are nearly cooked, add the tomato sauce and passata. Continue cooking for about 20 minutes. Remove some of the beans, blend until smooth, and return to the pan.

Cook the pasta in plenty of slightly salted boiling water for half its cooking time. Add to the beans to finish cooking in the soup for a few minutes until al dente. Let stand for 5 minutes before serving.

RAGÙ DI CARNE
Classic slow-cooked meat and tomato sauce

This rich *ragù* was originally created in the nineteenth century for Naples' noble families, a fact reflected in its use of meat and its more elaborate slow cooking method. It would certainly have been beyond the means of the city's poorer residents. Given the very long cooking time, it is a good idea to make the sauce the day before – the flavor only improves. The time and care devoted to preparing this dish led to its alternative name of *ragù*, or *sugo*, *della guardaporta* (doorkeeper's sauce), indicating the need for someone to watch over the pot while it cooked. It is actually two dishes in one: the meat is removed from the sauce and used as a main course, while the sauce is served with pasta.

✤ SERVES 4

2¼ lb beef, silverside or pork filets
  (ask your butcher for advice on the
  best cuts of beef)
3 teaspoons fresh flat-leaf parsley
  leaves, finely chopped
1¾ oz prosciutto crudo slices
2 tablespoons olive oil
1¾ oz lard
10 oz onions, chopped
1 or 2 garlic cloves, finely chopped
1 oz bacon fat
2 oz pancetta, chopped
4¼ cups dry red wine
10 oz passata
salt and freshly ground black pepper

First prepare the meat rolls. Take the beef, silverside or pork filets, and pound each one with a meat mallet or wooden rolling pin to flatten. Cover each filet with a sprinkling of parsley, then lay the prosciutto over the top. Season well with black pepper. Roll up and tie with butcher's string. Set aside.

Heat the oil and lard in a heavy saucepan over medium heat, and sweat the onions, garlic, bacon fat, and pancetta for a few minutes until the onion is soft and the pancetta is starting to brown. Add the meat rolls, cover the pan, and cook over gentle heat for about 5 minutes. When the onions start to turn golden brown, uncover the pan, and add the red wine. Continue cooking over gentle heat, stirring occasionally with a wooden spoon.

After a good hour, when all the liquid has reduced, add a little of the passata, stir, increase the heat slightly, and cook until the sauce has turned a rich, dark color. Add the rest of the passata, a little at a time. This process should take between 1½ to 2 hours. Add 2 cups of water, stir gently, and increase the heat to medium. Cover the pan and simmer gently (known as *pippiare* in Italian) for another 2 hours. When the meat is cooked through, remove from the sauce and transfer to a serving dish. Leave to rest in a warm place.

Continue simmering the *ragù* sauce until it is thick, dark, and glossy. Meanwhile, cook your preferred pasta in a large saucepan of slightly salted boiling water until al dente. Drain and add to the sauce. Toss through and serve as a first course. The meat is served with roast potatoes or a mixed green salad, or another vegetable side dish.

TUBETTI CON LE FAVE
Tubetti with fresh fava beans

Fresh fava beans are just one of the many vegetable crops with an important place in Campania's cuisine. At the beginning of the season, when they are at their most tender, they are often slipped out of their skins and eaten raw, dressed with seasoned olive oil. Later in the season they appear in stews and soups. In this dish from the region around Mount Vesuvius, renowned for the choice fava beans grown in its volcanic soil, the beans are first sweated gently, then cooked with the pasta, to produce a flavorful lunch or supper dish.

✣ SERVES 4

2 tablespoons olive oil
1 bunch of spring onions,
  finely chopped
2^1/$_2$ oz pancetta or bacon, diced
9 oz shelled fresh tender fava beans
10 oz tubetti rigati or similar large
  tube-shaped pasta such as ditali or
  pennette
handful of fresh flat-leaf parsley,
  leaves picked and chopped, to serve
salt and freshly ground black pepper
freshly grated pecorino cheese,
  to serve

Heat the olive oil in a large saucepan over medium heat, and gently sweat the spring onions, pancetta or bacon, and fava beans for a few minutes. Season well with salt and black pepper, and cook for 10–15 minutes until the beans are just tender (it is important not to let them become mushy). Add enough water to the pan to cook the pasta. When it comes to a rolling boil, add the tubetti and cook until al dente. Drain, transfer to a serving dish and sprinkle generously with the chopped parsley and plenty of freshly grated pecorino. Serve immediately.

LINGUINE CON FUNGHI E GAMBERONI
Linguine with mushrooms and jumbo shrimp

Mushrooms and jumbo shrimp combine perfectly in this simple but classic pasta dish, which is ideal for a quick lunch or supper. The recipe hails from the resort town of Castellammare di Stabia, situated on Campania's Sorrento Peninsula south of Naples and famed for its mineral springs.

✢ SERVES 4

2 tablespoons olive oil

2 garlic cloves, finely chopped

8–12 fresh raw jumbo shrimp, peeled and deveined

7 oz button mushrooms, finely sliced

3 1/2 oz Italian cooked ham, finely sliced

1 cup Cognac

2 cups dry white wine

1/3 cup good-quality vegetable stock

about 1/2 cup heavy cream

14 oz linguine

salt and freshly ground black pepper

generous handful of fresh flat-leaf parsley, chopped, to serve

Heat the oil in a large pan over medium-high heat, and sweat the garlic for a couple of minutes until starting to soften. Add the shrimp and season with salt and black pepper, sauté for a minute or so, then add the mushrooms and ham. Pour over the Cognac and allow it to reduce completely. Repeat the process with the white wine, until it has reduced as well. Next, pour in the stock and reduce the heat to medium. Continue cooking for another 10 minutes before adding the cream.

Meanwhile, cook the pasta in a large saucepan of slightly salted boiling water until al dente. Drain, adding to the shrimp and mushroom sauce after adding the cream. Increase the heat slightly, and quickly stir through to mix well. Serve hot, with a good sprinkling of chopped parsley over the top.

DI MUTUO SOCCORSO

CONCHIGLIE CON OLIO E LIMONE
Conchiglie with oil and lemon

Ideal on a hot summer's day, this cold pasta dish relies on using top-quality ingredients – pasta made from durum wheat, the finest extra virgin olive oil, and fragrant, juicy lemons. Lemons thrive in Campania's climate, and those from Sorrento, Capri, and Procida are particularly prized.

✣ SERVES 4

14 oz conchiglie (dried pasta shells)
extra virgin olive oil for drizzling
juice of 1 lemon
3 spring onions, green parts only,
  finely sliced on the diagonal
3 teaspoons fresh flat-leaf parsley
  leaves, finely chopped
salt and freshly ground black pepper

Cook the pasta in a large saucepan of slightly salted boiling water until al dente. Drain well. Place in a serving dish, drizzle with extra virgin olive oil, stir thoroughly and leave to cool. When the pasta is quite cold, pour over a little more olive oil, and season with salt and black pepper. Squeeze the lemon juice over the pasta and sprinkle with the spring onions and finely chopped parsley.

PASTA E ZUCCA
Pasta with pumpkin

The area surrounding Mount Vesuvius, with its fertile volcanic soil, produces lots of high-quality vegetables, and many recipes from the region make the most of what grows so well and abundantly. Choose a good variety of pumpkin for this dish, one with firm orange flesh and not too watery, to bring out the contrast between the creamy sweetness and the hint of chili.

✣ SERVES 4

olive oil
3 garlic cloves, finely chopped
2 1/4 lb pumpkin or butternut squash,
  peeled, seeds removed and cut into
  cubes
pinch of freshly grated nutmeg
1 fresh red chili, seeded and
  finely chopped
1 lb 2 oz tubetti
generous handful of fresh flat-leaf
  parsley, leaves picked and chopped
salt and freshly ground black pepper

Heat a generous amount of oil in a pan over medium heat. Add the garlic and sweat for a few minutes until soft and starting to caramelize. Add the diced pumpkin, nutmeg, and chili. Season with salt and black pepper. Pour in a little water, and cook over gentle heat for at least 15 minutes until the pumpkin breaks down into a thick, smooth sauce.

Cook the pasta in a large pan of slightly salted boiling water until al dente. Drain, saving a little of the cooking water. Add the pasta to the pumpkin sauce with a sprinkling of chopped parsley. Stir through. If the sauce is too dry, add a little of the reserved cooking water from the pasta to thin it slightly.

VERMICELLI AGLIO E OLIO
Vermicelli with garlic and oil

Simple but delicious – everything that embodies a dish from the *cucina povera* heritage. It is also very quick to make and requires only ingredients that you will almost always have on hand.

✢ SERVES 4

1 lb 5 oz vermicelli
3/4 cup olive oil
4 garlic cloves, finely chopped
3 fresh red chilies, seeded and finely
  chopped
handful of fresh flat-leaf parsley,
  leaves picked and chopped
salt and freshly ground black pepper

Cook the pasta in a large saucepan of slightly salted boiling water until al dente. While the pasta is cooking, heat the oil in a frying pan over medium heat, and sweat the garlic and chili (you do not want the garlic to brown and become bitter). When the garlic is soft and starts to caramelize, remove from the heat and add the parsley. Drain the pasta, transfer to a serving dish, and pour over the garlic oil. Stir well and serve immediately.

INSALATA DI RISO
Rice salad with tuna, eggs, and fontina

Readily meeting the *cucina povera* requirements of being filling and tasty, this rice salad is perfect for an al fresco lunch or even a picnic. It is worth buying tuna preserved in oil in a jar rather than a can, as the taste is far superior. Look for it in delicatessens and gourmet food shops.

✢ SERVES 4

1 lb 2 oz long-grain rice
4 tablespoons extra virgin olive oil,
  plus extra for drizzling
4 ripe salad tomatoes
2 tablespoons freshly squeezed
  lemon juice
2 or 3 large fresh basil leaves,
  finely sliced
7-oz jar tuna in oil, drained and
  broken up into flakes
1 3/4 oz green olives, pitted and halved
3 1/2 oz fontina cheese, diced
3 hard-boiled eggs, diced
salt and freshly ground black pepper

Cook the rice, drizzle with 2 tablespoons of extra virgin olive oil, stir well, and leave to cool.

Chop the tomatoes, drizzle with a little oil, and season with salt. Allow to sit for 5 minutes. Make a vinaigrette with 2 tablespoons of the extra virgin olive oil, lemon juice, and basil, and pour over the rice. Add all the other ingredients and mix well. Place in the refrigerator for 30 minutes or so, and serve chilled.

RISO BELLA NAPOLI
Creamy rice with fresh tomato and basil sauce

The tomato is so highly regarded in Campania that it should come as no surprise that it features in this Neapolitan version of risotto, which has its roots in the convent tradition. Unlike a risotto, the tomato sauce is made separately and stirred through once the rice is cooked.

✣ SERVES 4

3¹/₂ oz pancetta, diced

2 tablespoons olive oil

1 onion, finely chopped

1 lb 5 oz ripe tomatoes, peeled and chopped (see page 116)

4 or 5 large fresh basil leaves, torn

4 cups hot good-quality vegetable stock

2 oz butter

14 oz arborio or carnaroli rice

2 oz Parmesan cheese, grated

salt and freshly ground black pepper

Sweat the pancetta in the oil with half the onion over medium heat until the onion is soft and starts to caramelize. Add the tomatoes and basil, and season with salt and black pepper. Simmer gently for 30 minutes.

In the meantime, keep the stock hot in a saucepan for adding to the rice. Heat the butter in another saucepan and sweat the remaining onion until soft and starting to caramelize. Pour in a little of the stock while the onions are cooking. When the onions have reduced, add the rice, stir for a few minutes until the rice is coated in the butter, then pour in half the stock. Add the rest of the stock to the rice a little at a time, stirring continuously with a wooden spoon. Cook for about 20 minutes, stirring, until the rice is cooked but still has a slight bite and nearly all the stock has been absorbed. Add the tomato sauce and Parmesan cheese. Stir through to mix thoroughly, and let stand for a few minutes before serving.

SECONDI PIATTI
Main courses

PETTO DI POLLO AROMATICO
Spicy chicken roulades in tomato sauce

What little meat there is in much of Campania's regional cuisine usually comes from the historical elements that have had such a profound influence on the area's food: the royal and noble households of the French and Spanish courts, and the monasteries and convents. This recipe originates from the convents, and bears that unmistakable Campanian touch in its use of fresh herbs and a rich tomato sauce.

✛ SERVES 4

1 lb 2 oz chicken breast filet

2 or 3 stalks of fresh flat-leaf parsley,
 leaves picked and roughly chopped

1–2 garlic cloves, finely chopped

4 tablespoons freshly grated
 pecorino cheese

4 tablespoons freshly grated
 Parmesan cheese

small handful of fresh mint leaves,
 roughly chopped

2 whole fresh bay leaves,
 roughly chopped

1 teaspoon fresh rosemary leaves,
 chopped

1 fresh sage leaf, roughly chopped

2 tablespoons olive oil for cooking

1 cup dry white wine

1 lb 2 oz passata

1 fresh red chili, seeded and
 finely chopped

salt and freshly ground black pepper

small handful of large fresh basil
 leaves, rolled and finely sliced into
 chiffonade, to serve

To make the chicken roulades, slice each breast through the middle so that you are left with 2 thinner breasts. If you find it easier, or the breasts are not big enough, pound out the chicken using a meat mallet or wooden rolling pin, then cut each breast in half lengthwise. Trim the edges to neaten, if necessary. Lay out the slices of breast side by side on a work surface. Put a little parsley on each slice, saving some for later use, then divide up the garlic, pecorino, and Parmesan, and use to cover each slice. Season with salt and black pepper. Roll up the chicken into roulades, starting from one of the short edges, and secure with toothpicks or cocktail sticks.

Add the remaining parsley, the mint, bay leaves, rosemary, and sage to a heavy pan over medium heat with the oil. Quickly brown the roulades on all sides. When they are nicely browned, pour over the white wine and continue cooking for 20 minutes until the wine has reduced, turning the roulades from time to time. Add the passata, sprinkle in the chili and season with salt. Cover the pan and leave to simmer over low heat for 20 minutes. When the roulades are cooked, sprinkle with the basil and serve immediately, accompanied by a fresh green salad or a vegetable side dish such as lightly sautéed zucchinis.

TORTINO NAPOLETANO
Meatloaf with zucchini and mashed potato

The zucchinis used in this traditional convent recipe keep the meatloaf moist and soften the texture, while the smoked provolone melts into the meat beneath the fluffy potato topping.

✛ SERVES 4

1³/₄ oz butter plus extra for
  mashing and topping
2-3 tablespoons olive oil
2 onions, finely sliced
2¹/₄ lb lean ground beef
2¹/₄ lb starchy potatoes, such
  as russet
2¹/₄ lb zucchinis, sliced into rounds
1 garlic clove, finely chopped
a few fresh basil leaves, chopped
handful of dried breadcrumbs (see
  note on page 19)
5 oz provola affumicata (smoked
  provolone cheese), diced
salt and freshly ground black pepper

Preheat the oven to 325° (160°C). Heat the butter and oil in a heavy pan over medium heat, and sweat the onions for a few minutes until soft and starting to caramelize. Add the meat and brown, stirring frequently and using a wooden spoon to break up the meat. When the meat is nicely browned, remove from the heat and set aside.

Boil the potatoes with their skins on, peel, and mash. Add a little butter and salt. Using a clean pan, sauté the zucchinis and garlic in a little oil over medium heat for a few minutes until just starting to color. Stir in the basil, then add the zucchinis to the meat and stir through. Season with salt and black pepper.

Transfer the mixture to a buttered ovenproof dish and sprinkle with the breadcrumbs. Scatter over the diced provolone, cover with the mashed potato and dot with extra butter. Bake in the oven for 45 minutes. If the topping is starting to brown too much, cover the dish with foil – this will also help to keep the meatloaf moist. Cut into slices and serve.

FETTINE ALLA PIZZAIOLA
Slices of beef with tomato and oregano

Pizzaiola is a traditional Neapolitan tomato sauce seasoned with oregano that can also be used with pasta such as spaghetti or maccheroncelli. Here it is used to cover slices of beef, which are gently slow-cooked in the *pizzaiola* sauce to produce a meltingly tender, flavorful main course.

✛ SERVES 4

2 tablespoons olive oil
3 garlic cloves, finely chopped
2¹/₄ lb beef or veal scallops or thin,
  tender steaks such as sirloin
1 lb 2 oz ripe tomatoes, peeled,
  seeded, and chopped (see page 116)
1 tablespoon dried oregano
salt and freshly ground black pepper

Heat the oil in a large heavy pan over medium heat, and sweat the garlic for a few minutes until soft and translucent. Add the beef or veal and cook for 15 minutes until browned on both sides. Add the tomatoes and season with salt and black pepper. Crush the oregano lightly in the palm of your hand, then sprinkle over the top. Simmer over gentle heat for 45 minutes until the meat is very tender and the sauce has reduced and thickened. Serve the beef slices topped with the *pizzaiola* sauce.

CAPRETTO UOVA E FORMAGGIO
Braised kid with eggs and cheese

Kid meat is called *capretto* in Italy, and is far more tender than mature goat meat. Choose the tenderest cuts for this traditional Easter dish, preferably leg or loin, or even some parts of the shoulder or breast. If you cannot find kid, substitute with tender boned lamb.

✢ SERVES 4

3 lb 3 oz boned kid such as leg or loin

all-purpose flour for coating

2 tablespoons olive oil

2 garlic cloves, finely chopped

1 onion, finely chopped

1 lb 2 oz freshly shelled
  green peas

4 large eggs

pinch of salt

2 tablespoons freshly grated
  Parmesan cheese

juice of 1 lemon

salt and freshly ground black pepper

Clean the meat well, rinse, and pat dry with paper towels. Cut into large cubes and coat lightly in the flour. Heat the oil in a large heavy pan over medium heat and sweat the onion and garlic until soft and starting to caramelize. Remove a little of the onion mixture and set aside in a small pan for cooking the peas. Add the kid to the large pan and sauté for a few minutes until the meat is browned all over. Season with salt and black pepper. Add just enough water to keep the meat moist, and cook very slowly over a gentle heat for about 1 hour until the meat is tender. Keep adding a little water as necessary, so that the meat does not dry out.

About 15 minutes before the end of the cooking time, reheat the saved onion mixture over gentle heat. Add the peas and sweat for a few minutes, then put the contents of the pan into the meat. When the meat is ready, beat the eggs with a pinch of salt and the Parmesan. Pour into the pan and cook, stirring all the time, until all the meat is well coated (in a similar way to making spaghetti carbonara). Turn off the heat, quickly pour over the lemon juice, and stir through. Remove from the heat and serve immediately.

SPEZZATINO CON I PISELLI
Beef stew with peas and rosemary

Slow-cooking to bring flavor to the fore is a fundamental aspect of a number of traditional dishes in Campanian cuisine, such as this beef stew which came out of the convent kitchens.

✢ SERVES 4

1 oz butter

2 tablespoons olive oil

1 onion, roughly chopped

2¹/₄ lb stewing beef, cubed

2¹/₄ lb freshly shelled green peas

4 cups beef stock

3¹/₂ oz passata

3 teaspoons fresh rosemary leaves,
  chopped

salt and freshly ground black pepper

Heat the butter and oil in a heavy pan over medium heat and sweat the onion for a few minutes until soft and starting to caramelize. Add the meat and cook for 10 minutes until browned on all sides. Add the peas and continue cooking for a few minutes more.

Pour in the stock and passata, sprinkle in the rosemary, and season with salt and black pepper. Simmer very gently over medium heat, uncovered, for about 1 hour until the sauce has reduced and the meat is tender. Serve hot with mashed or roast potatoes.

REGIONAL WINEMAKING

After years of stagnation, Campanian wine production is now enjoying increasing success around the world. This is due to the introduction of new policies and to controls which balance the ever-increasing need for technological innovation with traditional methods. An increase in cellar facilities and new vineyard plantings are two direct results of this, as well as the adoption of more modern vinification techniques.

However, the region's winemakers have not only looked to the new in order to revitalize the industry and raise standards. Many plantings and replantings have actually been of old grape types that are particular to the region, drawing on Campania's highly distinctive wine heritage. Ancient vines such as Vitis Hellenica, Vitis Apiana and Vitis Aminea Gemina, as well as "timeless" wines such as Falerno, Faustiniano, and Caleno, are all individual enough to withstand the anonymous effects of the globalization of the wine market. In Campania, each wine is seen as a direct expression of the land, derived from both its geographical and its historical characteristics. Wine is seen as a kind of cultural ambassador – a banner where the landscape and the proverbial hospitality of its land of origin are inscribed.

Notable wineries, both large estates and family-owned businesses, include the relatively new Feudi di San Gregorio (producers of Taurasi and Greco di Tufo, among others), as well as Caggiano, Caputo, Maffini, Marisa Cuomo, Benito Ferraro, Mastroberardino, Mustilli, Villa Matilde, and Vestini Campagnano. If Feudi di San Gregorio can be seen as the new face of Campanian viticulture and winemaking, Mastroberardino perhaps represents both the traditional and the modern.

The Mastroberardino family has been making wine for more than 300 years. Committed to improving Campania's wine industry, the family firmly believes in taking advantage of new vinification techniques, while maintaining the history and cultural identity of Campanian wine. Mastroberardino has been responsible for much of the revival of Pompeiian vineyards, growing grape varieties such as Fiano, Greco di Tufo, and Aglianico, and produces very good Taurasi. Similar family-owned ventures such as Villa Matilde, responsible for much of the Falerno grape's rejuvenation, and Mustilli, which grows Greco, Falanghina, Piedirosso, and Aglianico, also carry the torch for Campanian wine tradition.

BRACIOLONE ALLA NAPOLETANA
Pork roulade with prosciutto, Parmesan, and parsley

✣ SERVES 4–6

2³/₄ lb pork filet or boned
   shoulder of pork

7 oz lean ground pork

5 oz prosciutto or pancetta, chopped

1 oz Parmesan cheese, grated

1³/₄ oz golden raisins

1³/₄ oz pine nuts

1 hard-boiled egg, chopped

1 garlic clove, finely chopped

handful of fresh flat-leaf parsley,
   leaves picked and chopped

1³/₄ oz dried breadcrumbs (see note
   on page 19)

1 tablespoon olive oil

1³/₄ oz lard

1 onion, cut into fine wedges

2 cups red wine

1 lb 2 oz ripe tomatoes, peeled, seeded,
   and diced (see note on page 116)

pinch of sugar (optional)

salt and freshly ground black pepper

Cut the meat into thin slices lengthwise. (Alternatively, you can slit the pork lengthwise down the middle, about halfway through.) Using a smooth meat mallet or wooden rolling pin, pound the meat to flatten slightly if necessary. Trim away any rough edges to neaten. Arrange the pieces in a row one next to the other, slightly overlapping the edges. Make a stuffing using the ground pork, prosciutto or pancetta, Parmesan, golden raisins, pine nuts, hard-boiled egg, garlic, parsley, and breadcrumbs. Season with salt and black pepper. Combine all the ingredients thoroughly, and spread the stuffing over the meat. Roll the meat up firmly like a Swiss roll and tie in place with butcher's string, securing in enough places along the length of the roulade to keep the meat in a tight roll and the stuffing in place. Also tie at each end like a sausage so that the stuffing doesn't ooze out.

Heat the oil and lard in a deep-sided heavy frying pan over medium heat. Brown the roulade on all sides with the onion – you want the meat to color before it starts cooking in the sauce. Pour over the red wine and allow to reduce for 10 minutes. Add the tomatoes, cover the pan, and cook for about an hour, turning the meat from time to time. Towards the end of the cooking time, season the sauce with salt and black pepper, and if necessary a little sugar to cut the tartness of the tomatoes. Cut the pork into thick slices and serve with green beans and roast potatoes, or other vegetable side dishes.

SALSICCE DEL PRETE
Pan-fried sausages with new potatoes and chili

As the literal name of this recipe – priest's sausages – suggests, this is another dish that emerged from the monasteries and convents of Campania.

✣ SERVES 4

2 tablespoons lard or olive oil

1 lb 2 oz new potatoes, unpeeled and sliced

1 fresh red chili, seeded and finely chopped

2¼ lb fresh Italian pork sausages

salt and freshly ground black pepper

Heat half the lard or oil in a frying pan over medium heat. Add the potatoes and sauté for 20 minutes. Meanwhile, in a separate pan, heat the remaining lard or oil. Add the chili and a good grinding of black pepper and finally the sausages. Fry for about 15 minutes until the sausages are well browned. Once the potatoes are cooked, put into the same pan as the sausages. Stir through gently and serve immediately.

SALSICCE AL CARTOCCIO
Charcoal-grilled sausages in a parcel

In culinary terms, *al cartoccio* means to cook something in a wrapper – in this case foil-wrapped sausages which are grilled in the hot charcoal of a barbecue. This cooking method imparts an intriguing smoky element to the flavorful herby sausages used in this traditional dish from the Campanian countryside.

✣ SERVES 4

1 tablespoon lard or olive oil

2¼ lb fresh Italian fennel sausages or similar

Heat a charcoal barbecue or grill until the charcoal is white-hot. Take some pieces of foil and grease with the lard or oil. Arrange the sausages in pairs on each piece of foil and wrap tightly. Carefully place in the hot charcoal ashes and leave the sausages to grill for about 30 minutes, making sure that they do not char or burn. Remove from the charcoal using a pair of tongs, carefully unwrap the foil, and serve the sausages hot, with the vegetable side dishes of your choice as an accompaniment.

SALSICCE ALLA CONTADINA
Country-style sausages with lentils

A traditional dish from the countryside surrounding Naples, this one features lentils. Legumes are an important staple in much of the regional cuisine, particularly in those dishes that fall into the category of *cucina povera*.

✛ SERVES 4

2 garlic cloves
14 oz brown lentils, picked and rinsed
2 tablespoons olive oil
1 carrot, roughly chopped
1 celery stick, roughly chopped
2¹/₄ lb fresh Italian pork sausages
14 oz ripe tomatoes, peeled, seeded,
  and chopped (see note on page 116)
salt and freshly ground black pepper

Roughly chop 1 clove of the garlic. Put in a pan with the lentils, cover with water, and bring to a boil over medium heat. Simmer for 20 minutes, then remove from the heat but do not drain.

Meanwhile, finely chop the remaining clove of garlic. Heat the oil in a heavy frying pan over medium heat. Sweat the chopped garlic, carrot, and celery for a few minutes until soft. Add the sausages and brown in the pan, then add the tomatoes. Continue cooking for about 15 minutes until the tomatoes have broken down and the sauce has thickened. Add the lentils with their cooking liquid, and season with salt and black pepper. Simmer gently for another 15 minutes. Serve hot.

CONIGLIO ALLA NONNA RITA
Braised rabbit with onions and brandy

Ischia Porto is one of two distinct districts that make up Ischia, the major town on the volcanic island of the same name. It grew up around the island's main harbor, and the dockside restaurants and bars readily attract the streams of visitors traveling to and fro. This recipe was created for Ischia Porto's Nonna Rita restaurant.

✢ SERVES 4

2 tablespoons olive oil
1 rabbit, about 2¼ lb
2 garlic cloves, finely chopped
1 fresh red chili, seeded and
 finely chopped
1 cup of brandy or white wine
2¼ lb onions, sliced
2 or 3 ripe tomatoes, peeled, seeded,
 and chopped
1 whole bay leaf (fresh if possible)
2–3 teaspoons fresh rosemary leaves
salt

Clean the rabbit and cut into pieces, making sure that you remove the gland at the bottom of the spine. Heat the oil in a heavy frying pan over medium heat and sauté the rabbit pieces for 10 minutes until nicely browned, cooking in batches if necessary. Return all the rabbit to the pan and add the garlic and chili. Sweat for a few minutes until soft and starting to caramelize.

Pour in the brandy or wine, and allow to reduce for 5 minutes. Add the onions, tomatoes, bay leaf, and rosemary. Season with salt. Add a little water if necessary – just enough to keep the sauce moist. Cover the pan and cook for about an hour, stirring occasionally and keeping an eye on the sauce to make sure it doesn't dry out (add more water as necessary). Slow-cooking rabbit in this way helps to keep it tender and moist. Serve hot with roast potatoes or other vegetable side dishes. You could also use the sauce to serve with pasta such as penne or vermicelli.

CONIGLIO ALL'ISCHITANA
Braised rabbit with wine, tomato, and herbs

Rabbit is a specialty on Ischia, so much so that old and long-revered techniques for breeding are still practised by the island's farmers. The rabbits are raised in ditches until they are fully grown, to produce the best possible meat. This recipe is a traditional one.

✢ SERVES 4

1 rabbit, about 2¼ lb
2 tablespoons olive oil
1 teaspoon fresh rosemary leaves
about 2 cups dry white wine
1 lb 2 oz ripe tomatoes, peeled,
 seeded, and chopped
2 or 3 large fresh basil leaves,
 chopped
salt and freshly ground black pepper

Clean the rabbit and cut into pieces, making sure that you remove the gland at the bottom of the spine. Heat the oil in a heavy pan over medium heat. Add the rabbit and rosemary and sauté for 10 minutes until the rabbit is nicely browned all over. Pour over the white wine and leave to reduce completely, before adding the tomato and basil. Season with salt and black pepper, and stir through.

Cover the pan and braise the rabbit for about an hour, stirring occasionally and adding a little more wine and just enough water to keep the meat moist. Increase the heat for a few minutes, turning the rabbit pieces to give them an even flavor. Serve immediately.

SCALOPPINE DI MONTAGNA
Veal scallops with prosciutto, capers, and mushrooms

Gutsy flavors and hearty ingredients are trademarks of dishes from the mountain regions of Campania, reflecting the strength of the people who made their lives in this rugged environment.

✣ SERVES 4

2¹/₄ lb veal scallops
all-purpose flour for coating
3¹/₂ oz prosciutto crudo slices
1 lb 2 oz ripe tomatoes, sliced
3–4 teaspoons salted capers, rinsed
  and gently squeezed dry
5 oz Italian mushrooms in oil
2 tablespoons chopped fresh oregano
2 tablespoons chopped fresh
  flat-leaf parsley
2 tablespoons chopped fresh basil
olive oil for drizzling
salt and freshly ground black pepper

Preheat the oven to 325°F (160°C). If the veal is not already flattened, use a smooth meat mallet or wooden rolling pin to pound the veal lightly to an even thickness. Heat a lightly oiled ridged grill pan or griddle over medium-high heat. Coat the veal in the flour, shaking off any excess. Quickly sear the veal in the pan for a couple of minutes on both sides.

Transfer to an oiled baking dish, arranging the pieces of veal side by side. Place slices of prosciutto, slices of tomato, some capers, and mushrooms on each one. Season with salt and a little pepper. Sprinkle with oregano, parsley, and basil, and drizzle with oil. Cover the dish with foil and bake in the oven for 15–20 minutes, removing the foil halfway through cooking. Serve immediately.

LE FETTINE DI PULCINELLA
Veal in white wine with cherry tomatoes and mushrooms

Pulcinella, a popular figure in Neapolitan puppetry, gives his name to this *cucina povera* dish.

✣ SERVES 4

1 lb 2 oz veal scallops
all-purpose flour for coating
a little olive oil
2 cups dry white wine
10 oz cherry tomatoes
3¹/₂ oz Italian cooked ham, chopped
3¹/₂ oz button mushrooms, sliced
salt and freshly ground black pepper
handful of fresh flat-leaf parsley,
  chopped, to garnish

If the veal is not already flattened, use a smooth meat mallet or wooden rolling pin to pound the veal lightly to an even thickness. Coat the veal in the flour, shaking off any excess. Heat a little olive oil in a large heavy pan over medium heat, add the veal, and brown for a minute or two on each side. Add the white wine and allow to reduce for 10 minutes.

Gently crush the cherry tomatoes and add to the pan with the ham and mushrooms. Season with salt and black pepper and allow to cook gently for 30 minutes. Sprinkle with chopped parsley and serve immediately.

POLPETTE ALLA NAPOLETANA
Meatballs in tomato sauce

Polpette (meatballs) and *polpettone* (meatloaf) feature throughout Italian cuisine. In this version from Campania's convent tradition, naturally enough the juicy meatballs are cooked in a rich tomato sauce. The meatloaf below is also a convent recipe, and has a scamorza cheese filling. Scamorza is made from cow's milk and is similar in many ways to mozzarella. It melts far better when baked, however, and its smoked version adds a lovely depth of flavor.

⁘ SERVES 4

1 lb 2 oz stale crustless bread such as
   ciabatta or pane casereccio
a little milk
1 lb 2 oz lean ground beef
handful of fresh flat-leaf parsley,
   leaves picked and chopped
1 garlic clove, finely chopped
1 large egg, lightly beaten
1¾ oz freshly grated Parmesan cheese
1½ oz golden raisins (optional)
1½ oz pine nuts (optional)
light olive oil for cooking
1 small onion, finely chopped
1 lb 5 oz canned whole peeled plum
   tomatoes
salt and freshly ground black pepper

Soak the bread in a little milk. Squeeze gently to remove any excess liquid and place in a bowl with the ground beef, parsley, and garlic. Mix well and add the egg, a pinch of salt, black pepper, Parmesan, golden raisins, and pine nuts (if using). Combine thoroughly with your hands. Shape into meatballs, and fry in plenty of hot oil in a large heavy pan over medium heat for 10 minutes. Keep turning the meatballs carefully to prevent them from sticking to the bottom of the pan. Remove from the pan, drain on kitchen paper and set aside.

Meanwhile, make the tomato sauce. Sweat the onion in a little olive oil in a heavy pan over medium heat until soft and translucent. Add the tomatoes and season with salt and black pepper. Transfer the meatballs to the sauce and cook for 10 minutes to heat through. Serve hot.

Polpettone – meatloaf with prosciutto, scamorza, and Parmesan
Preheat the oven to 350°F (180°C). Soak 1 lb 2 oz bread in 4 cups milk, drain and squeeze the bread gently to remove any excess liquid. Put in a bowl with 1 lb 2 oz lean ground beef or pork, 2 eggs, 1 finely chopped garlic clove, 1 tablespoon freshly grated Parmesan cheese, and a handful of chopped fresh flat-leaf parsley leaves. Season well with salt and freshly ground black pepper. Combine thoroughly with your hands, and pat out into a rectangle about 1 inch thick.

Cut 3½ oz prosciutto and 2 oz smoked scamorza cheese into thin strips, and arrange over the ground meat mixture. Put 2 whole hard-boiled eggs on top and wrap the meat around the eggs, shaping it into a meatloaf. (This is easier if your hands are wet.) Carefully transfer to an oiled baking dish – you'll need one larger than the meatloaf, so that you will be able to turn the loaf during cooking. Bake in the preheated oven for 40 minutes, turning from time to time. Cut into slices and serve hot.

INSALATA DI CARNE
Arugula salad with warm grilled beef, cherry tomatoes, and basil

A perfect dish for al fresco dining, this salad works beautifully as part of a selection of dishes for a lunch for family or friends. It is a classic summertime dish that is very popular in Naples. Choose the ripest, sweetest cherry tomatoes you can find.

✛ SERVES 4–6

2¼ lb beef filet or similar tender cut
   of beef
olive oil for grilling
3½ oz young arugula leaves (if you
   use larger arugula leaves, tear
   before using)
1 lb 2 oz ripe cherry tomatoes, halved
a few fresh basil leaves, chopped
2 garlic cloves, finely chopped
a little extra virgin olive oil
salt and freshly ground black pepper

Rub the beef filet all over with olive oil and season well on all sides with salt and black pepper. Heat a ridged grill pan or heavy frying pan over medium-high heat and add the beef. Grill for 20–25 minutes, turning occasionally to brown all over, until the beef is well cooked (if you prefer your meat to be a little pink in the middle, simply cook for slightly less time). Let sit for a few minutes.

Meanwhile, put the arugula, tomatoes, basil, and garlic in a large bowl. Season with salt and black pepper and drizzle with a little extra virgin olive oil. Cut the meat into slices and arrange on a serving platter. Arrange the salad over the top and serve immediately.

BACCALÀ IN PASTELLA
Battered salt cod filets

Baccalà, or salt cod, is popular across much of the Mediterranean, in Portugal, Spain, and Italy. Naples is no exception, where it was embraced as part of *cucina povera* because it was cheap, readily available, and kept for such a long time.

✛ SERVES 4

9 oz all-purpose flour
1 oz fresh yeast
pinch of salt
¼ cup hot water
1 lb 5 oz salt cod, soaked in several
   changes of cold water for 24 hours
vegetable oil for deep-frying
salt and freshly ground black pepper

Make a batter with the flour, yeast, a pinch of salt, and the hot water. Mix vigorously, cover, and let rise for 30 minutes in a warm, dry place.

In the meantime, rinse the salt cod and remove the bones and skin. Put in a saucepan with plenty of water and bring to a boil. Reduce the heat and simmer for about 10 minutes. Drain well, then break up the salt cod into flakes and add to the batter.

Heat enough oil for deep-frying in a high-sided heavy pan until very hot. Drop in spoonfuls of the salt cod batter. Serve the fritters piping hot with a sprinkling of salt and black pepper.

ALICI RIPIENE
Boned and stuffed anchovies

Fresh anchovies deteriorate quickly, so if you do not live beside the sea where these prized little fish are caught, you may be out of luck. If you cannot find fresh anchovies, you can buy unsalted anchovies already fileted and preserved in oil – try your local fish dealer. In this typical family recipe from the Sorrento coast, the fresh tang of the stuffing contrasts wonderfully with the crisp battered fish.

❖ SERVES 4

2¹/₄ lb fresh anchovy filets
4 garlic cloves, finely chopped
handful of fresh flat-leaf parsley,
  roughly chopped
1³/₄ oz pecorino cheese, grated
all-purpose flour for coating
5 eggs, beaten
oil for frying
salt and freshly ground black pepper
3 lemons, cut into wedges, to serve

Rinse the anchovies and slit in half lengthwise. Remove the bones and rinse the anchovy halves. Lay half of the anchovies skin-side down on a working surface. Make a stuffing by combining the garlic, parsley, and cheese. Season with salt and black pepper. Spread a little of the stuffing over each anchovy, then cover each one with one of the remaining anchovy halves, skin-side up, to make little "sandwiches." Press down well.

Heat enough oil for shallow-frying in a heavy frying pan over medium heat. When the oil is the correct temperature, coat the anchovy sandwiches in a little flour, then dip in the beaten eggs. Carefully lower into the pan, and shallow-fry on both sides in the hot oil, cooking in batches if necessary. Cook for 15–20 minutes until the skin is crisp and the fish is just cooked through. Serve immediately, with the lemon wedges for squeezing over the top.

FROM THE SEA

A wealth of fantastic fish and seafood is found all along Campania's coastline, drawn from the Tyrrhenian Sea and the Bay of Naples. Long a source of food for the region's inhabitants, the bounty of the sea has become an intrinsic part of its distinctive cuisine. Red mullet, grey mullet, sea bream, tuna, anchovies, sardines, mackerel, clams, mussels, cuttlefish, squid, octopus – all these and more make their way from fishermen's nets and baskets to the fish markets and then onto the dining table. Yet even here, in the past, a clear division could be seen between the food of the rich and the poor. While the noble and wealthy families dined on the more prized white fish, such as red mullet and bream, and shellfish, such as oysters, poorer inhabitants made the most of what was considered to be inferior.

Clams, mussels, grey mullet, anchovies, and sardines, among others, became characteristic and much-loved ingredients of *cucina povera*. Today, what began as necessity is now very much a proud tradition; fish and seafood that were once chosen because of financial hardship are now eaten not only because of historical and cultural tradition, but also because of their quality and flavor. On any given day in the fish markets, you will find eager and discerning

customers carefully making their selections, inspecting and questioning to make sure that they are buying the freshest squid or the firmest fish.

There was another historical division in the food, though, and that was between sea and land. Certainly, fish and seafood were staples of the diet for island and coastal dwellers. Away from the coast, however, it was a different story. In the mountains of Benevento and Avellino, for instance, seafood hardly appeared in the diet at all, except in the form of preserved fish such as anchovies or *baccalà* (salt cod). Perhaps this is one of the reasons why, even in times of modern refrigeration, salt cod is still widely eaten throughout Campania even though it is now relatively easy to buy fresh fish. Salt cod at Christmas is a tradition that continues to this day.

A common thread running throughout the preparation of fish is simplicity. Fresh fish, such as bream, tend to be baked or grilled whole and are simply dressed with olive oil, garlic, and parsley. The same applies to seafood, such as mussels and clams. Even when ingredients like tomatoes appear, they never overwhelm the dish, allowing the flavor of the seafood to shine through.

FRITTURA DI CALAMARI E SCAMPI
Fried squid and scampi

Although sometimes synonymous with shrimp, scampi are actually a type of lobster; in cooking, scampi generally refers to the peeled tail section. If you cannot find scampi for this traditional Neapolitan dish, substitute whole shrimp instead, deveined but with the unpeeled tail left intact.

✤ SERVES 4

1 lb 2 oz squid
1 lb 2 oz scampi, such as Norway
  lobster or Dublin Bay prawns,
  or substitute whole shrimp
all-purpose flour for coating
vegetable oil for frying
salt and freshly ground black pepper
lemon wedges, to serve

Clean the squid and cut into rings (see page 16). Wash and clean the scampi. Coat the squid and scampi in flour, shaking off any excess. Heat plenty of oil for deep-frying in a large frying pan over medium heat. Carefully drop in the squid and scampi, cooking in batches so that you do not crowd the pan. Fry for 5 minutes until golden. Drain on paper towels and sprinkle with salt and black pepper. Serve piping hot, with lemon wedges for squeezing over the top.

SOUTÈ DI VONGOLE
Clams sautéed in garlic and oil

Another classic Neapolitan recipe, this one uses the abundant clams found along Campania's coastline.

✤ SERVES 4

4 1/2 lb carpet shell clams
2 tablespoons olive oil
5 garlic cloves, finely chopped
generous handful of fresh flat-leaf
  parsley, chopped
salt and freshly ground black pepper

Rinse the clams and leave to soak in salted water for a few hours to release any grit (see note on page 42). Rinse well under cold running water. Tap on a work surface and discard any that do not close or have broken shells.

Heat the oil in a heavy saucepan over medium heat and sweat the garlic for a few minutes until soft and starting to caramelize. Add the clams and a good sprinkling of black pepper. Cover the pan and sauté the clams, shaking the pan occasionally until they open (discard any that do not open). Transfer to a serving bowl, sprinkle the clams generously with chopped parsley, and serve immediately.

CEFALO ARROSTO
Grilled marinated grey mullet

Grey mullet is a popular catch in the Bay of Naples, and this traditional fisherman's recipe is typical of those from the Borgo Santa Lucia area of Naples, the city's old fishing quarter.

✤ SERVES 4

4½ lb whole grey mullet
2 tablespoons olive oil
1–2 tablespoons balsamic vinegar
4 garlic cloves, finely chopped
handful of fresh flat-leaf parsley,
  leaves picked and chopped
2 fresh sage leaves, chopped
2 teaspoons fresh rosemary leaves,
  chopped
5 slices crustless stale Italian bread
  such as ciabatta or pane casereccio,
  broken up into large crumbs
salt
3 lemons, cut into slices, to serve

Clean the fish and cut a slit through the belly. Remove the innards and the bones (you can ask your fish dealer to do this). Combine the oil, vinegar, garlic, parsley, sage, and rosemary in a small bowl. Drench the bread in the herb mixture. Stuff the cavity in each fish with the bread mixture and secure with a toothpick or cocktail stick.

Heat a barbecue or charcoal grill, or a ridged grill pan, until medium hot. Arrange the fish on the grill and cook, brushing continually with the excess marinade and turning frequently, for 25–30 minutes. Be careful not to overcook. Serve the fish with slices of lemon.

CEFALO ALLA MARINARA
Grey mullet with spring onions and parsley

Given its long history, it is only natural that most dishes originating in Borgo Santa Lucia center on the bounty of the sea. Once again, grey mullet is the fish of choice, but this time it is cooked whole in a simple fresh herb sauce.

✤ SERVES 4

4½ lb whole grey mullet
1 tablespoon olive oil
1 lb 2 oz spring onions,
  green part only, finely sliced on
  the diagonal
generous handful fresh flat-leaf
  parsley, leaves picked and roughly
  chopped
salt and freshly ground black pepper

Clean the fish (you can ask your fish dealer to do this) and arrange in a heavy frying pan. Drizzle with the oil, then sprinkle the spring onions and parsley over the fish. Season with salt and black pepper. Add 1 cup water and simmer over gentle heat for 30 minutes until the fish is cooked through. Add a little extra water if necessary, as the fish is cooking, to keep it from drying out. Serve hot, with the fish juices served separately.

TRIGLIE DEL PESCATORE
Grilled marinated red mullet

Red mullet is a delicate, flaky fish that works very well when grilled or barbecued. Marinating the fish before grilling, then basting again with the marinade during the cooking process, improves its flavor even more. This time the recipe comes from Borgo Marinari, a traditional fishing village in the old Santa Lucia quarter sitting right on the water's edge.

✣ SERVES 4

4 tablespoons olive oil

3 garlic cloves, finely chopped

generous handful of fresh flat-leaf parsley, roughly chopped

juice of 2 lemons plus 1 tablespoon extra for grilling

6 whole red mullet, cleaned (you can ask your fish dealer to do this)

2 or 3 fresh mint leaves, chopped

salt and freshly ground black pepper

Prepare a marinade with half of the oil, the garlic, parsley, and juice of 2 lemons. Season well with salt and black pepper. Lay the fish in a single layer in a shallow glass or ceramic dish and leave to marinate in the refrigerator for at least an hour.

Heat a ridged grill pan or heavy frying pan over medium heat. Make a separate marinade for brushing the fish with the remaining oil, the extra lemon juice, and the mint. Season with salt and black pepper. Once the pan is hot, grill the fish for 3–4 minutes on each side until just cooked through, brushing frequently with the marinade. (Be careful not to overcook; otherwise the flesh will be dry.) Serve immediately.

Note If you choose to barbecue the fish or cook them over a charcoal grill, you may find it easier to use a wire fish rack to cook them in, as these fish are so delicate. This helps to prevent them breaking up or losing their tails.

SPIGOLA AL FORNO
Baked sea bass with oil and lemon

Sea bass is another typical fish found in Naples' markets and fish dealers. In this recipe, it is treated with the simple reverence that is fundamental in so much of Neapolitan cuisine.

✣ SERVES 4

3 garlic cloves, finely chopped

handful of fresh flat-leaf parsley, leaves picked and chopped

2 tablespoons olive oil

1 large sea bass (about 2¾ lb) or 2 small ones, cleaned and scaled

juice of 2 lemons

salt

Preheat the oven to 300° (150°C). In a small bowl, mix the garlic and parsley with half the oil. Season with salt and use the mixture to stuff the fish. Place in a fish pan, and drizzle with the remaining oil. Bake in the oven for 15 minutes, then add the lemon juice. Bake for another 15 minutes, transfer to a serving platter, and serve hot.

SEPPIE IMBOTTITE

Squid stuffed with shellfish and bread

You would expect a dish from Naples' Borgo Marinari district to make the very best of a fisherman's daily catch. On almost any given day, if you walk down to the shoreline in Naples, you will find fishermen sorting and selling fish and seafood straight from the sea – and often still wriggling, which is a guarantee of freshness. The squid used in this recipe is kept moist and succulent as it cooks by the seafood-studded bread stuffing, then smothered in a smooth chili-spiked tomato sauce.

⊹ SERVES 4

6 large squid
4 tablespoons olive oil
1 lb 2 oz raw shrimp, peeled and
  deveined
2 eggs
1 tablespoon freshly grated
  pecorino cheese
1 lb 2 oz stale good-quality bread
  such as ciabatta or pane casereccio,
  crusts removed
1 fresh red chili, seeded and
  finely chopped
2 garlic cloves, finely chopped
1³/4 lb ripe tomatoes, peeled and
  chopped
salt and freshly ground black pepper
generous handful of fresh flat-leaf
  parsley, leaves picked and chopped,
  to serve

Clean the squid well, removing the eyes, ink sacs, and beaks (see page 16) so that you are left with a long tube. Heat 2 tablespoons of the oil in a heavy frying pan over medium heat and sauté the shrimp for 5–8 minutes, depending on size, until they turn pink and opaque. Remove from the pan, chop into small pieces and set aside in a bowl.

Soak the bread in a little water, then gently squeeze out any excess liquid. Whisk the eggs with the pecorino and bread. Season with salt and black pepper, and add to the shrimp. Mix the filling well and use it to stuff the squid. Tie up the open ends with butcher's string or cotton thread.

Heat the remaining oil in a large heavy pan over medium heat and sweat the garlic with the chili for a few minutes until soft and starting to caramelize. Add the squid and quickly sauté until golden brown, then add the tomatoes, cover the pan, and leave for 20 minutes to cook through, stirring occasionally. Remove the squid from the pan, snip off the string, and set aside. Quickly push the tomato sauce through a sieve to ensure it is smooth. Serve the stuffed squid hot, cut into slices, accompanied by the tomato sauce and a good sprinkling of chopped parsley.

BACCALÀ ALLA NAPOLETANA
Salt cod filets with tomato, olives, and capers

The classic Neapolitan triumvirate of tomatoes, olives, and capers adds its characteristic piquancy to this simple dish, as well as providing layers of texture and depth.

✛ SERVES 4

2¹/₄ lb salt cod

4 tablespoons olive oil

3 garlic cloves, finely chopped

1 lb 2 oz ripe tomatoes, peeled, seeded, and chopped (see note on page 116)

5 oz black olives, pitted and left whole or halved

1³/₄ oz salted capers, rinsed and gently squeezed dry

all-purpose flour for coating

generous handful of fresh flat-leaf parsley, leaves picked and chopped

salt and freshly ground black pepper

Soak the salt cod in several changes of cold fresh water overnight.

The next day, preheat the oven to 300 (150°C). Heat half of the oil in a large heavy pan over medium heat. Sweat the garlic for a few minutes until soft and starting to color. Using a slotted spoon, remove the garlic from the pan, leaving the oil behind. Add the tomatoes, olives, and capers. Season with a little salt and a generous grinding of black pepper. Cook over gentle heat for 10–15 minutes until the tomatoes start to break down.

In the meantime, drain the salt cod and rinse well under cold running water. Remove and discard any bones or skin, then pat the salt cod dry with paper towels. Cut into pieces and coat in a little flour. Heat the remaining oil in a separate large heavy pan over medium heat and quickly fry the cod until golden on all sides. Remove from the pan with a slotted spoon and drain on paper towels.

Return the cod to the same pan as the tomato mixture and sprinkle in the parsley. Cook for a few more minutes, then transfer to an ovenproof dish and bake in the preheated oven for 10 minutes. Serve hot.

BACCALÀ ALLA FRANCESE
Salt cod with onion and wine

Mussillo is a whole piece of salt cod taken from the center of the fish. It is left whole and gently simmered in the onion and wine sauce until tender.

✛ SERVES 4

2¹/₄ lb mussillo of salt cod (the center cut of the cod)

1 onion, sliced

2 tablespoons olive oil

pinch of salt

2 cups dry white wine

8 cups boiling water

generous handful of fresh flat-leaf parsley, leaves picked and chopped

freshly ground black pepper

Soak the salt cod in several changes of cold fresh water overnight.

The next day, rinse the salt cod well under running water, pat dry with paper towels, and put in a large heavy pan with the onion, oil, and a pinch of salt. Season with black pepper. Sweat over medium heat for about 10 minutes, turning the cod over halfway during cooking. Pour wine over the cod and cook for another 5 minutes until the wine has reduced completely.

Add the boiling water and simmer gently, uncovered, for 30 minutes. When the fish looks tender, add a good sprinkling of chopped parsley, cook for another 5 minutes, and serve hot.

BOCCONCINI DEL PRETE
Baked mini omelettes with provolone, ham, and tomato

Bocconcini means "delicacies" – in this case, priests' delicacies. This is another convent recipe that makes the most of a few premium ingredients. Here, the sweet, acidic intensity of the tomato topping cuts through the richness of the provolone cheese and ham to provide a perfect balance.

✤ SERVES 4

1 lb 9 oz canned whole peeled plum
  tomatoes
2 tablespoons olive oil
1³/₄ oz dried oregano
12 eggs
3¹/₂ oz Parmesan cheese, grated
7 oz Italian cooked ham, sliced
7 oz provola affumicata (smoked
  provolone cheese), sliced
salt and freshly ground black pepper

Preheat the oven to 300 (150°C). Roughly chop the tomatoes and put in a pan with their juices. Add a little oil and the oregano and season with salt and black pepper. Cook gently over medium heat, stirring occasionally, until the tomatoes break up and reduce into a thick sauce.

Beat the eggs with a little salt and the Parmesan. Place a small omelette pan or similar over medium heat and make 8 small equal-sized omelettes using the egg mixture. (If you do not have a pan that is small enough, you could use an extra-large round biscuit cutter about 4 inches or so in diameter to contain your omelettes initially, while they start to set.) Do not fold over and do not allow the egg to set completely. Carefully slide them out of the pan with a spatula and arrange four of the omelettes side by side in a baking dish. Put some ham and provolone on top of each one and cover with another little omelette, then pour over the tomato sauce. Bake in the oven for a few minutes until the cheese starts to melt. Serve hot.

FRITTO DI MOZZARELLA E PROVOLA
Mozarella and provolone fritters

Provolone is considered a Southern Italian cheese, even if today much of it is produced in the north of the country. It makes the perfect companion for that quintessentially Campanian cheese, mozzarella, in these traditional fritters that are often sold as street food in Naples.

✤ SERVES 4

9 oz buffalo mozzarella cheese, cut
  into slices
9 oz provola affumicata (smoked
  provolone cheese), sliced
all-purpose flour for coating
9 oz good-quality dried breadcrumbs
  (see note on page 19)
vegetable oil for shallow-frying

Coat the mozzarella and provolone slices in flour, then dip in beaten egg, and finally, in breadcrumbs.

Heat enough oil for shallow-frying in a heavy pan over medium heat. When the oil is hot, shallow-fry the cheese fritters for about 5 minutes until the coating is crisp and golden and the cheese is melting inside. Carefully turn halfway during the cooking time using an spatula, then lift out of the pan to drain briefly on paper towels once cooked. It is important to serve these virtually straight from the frying pan to the table – *frienn' magnann'* – with a warning to guests about the hot cheese inside.

FRITTATA DI PATATE
Potato frittata

Frittate make a perfect family meal or easy lunch or supper dish, and they really could not be easier to make. Three recipes for frittata are actually given here, and all make use of simple but high-quality produce for the best results.

⊹ SERVES 4

1 tablespoon olive oil
2^1/$_4$ lb low-starch potatoes, such as yellow finn, peeled and cut into cubes
8 large eggs
2 cups milk
1–2 tablespoons freshly grated Parmesan cheese plus extra for sprinkling (optional)
generous handful of fresh flat-leaf parsley, leaves picked and chopped
3^1/$_2$ oz butter
salt and freshly ground black pepper

Heat the oil in a large frying pan over medium heat and sauté the potatoes for 15 minutes until golden. Don't cook completely – just until they start to color and soften slightly inside (otherwise they will break up when you add them to the frittata mixture). Drain on paper towels and leave to cool.

In the meantime, put the eggs, milk, 1–2 tablespoons Parmesan cheese, and the parsley in a large bowl. Season with salt and black pepper and whisk until the mixture is well combined and the eggs are light and fluffy. Add the potato and gently stir through to mix well.

To cook the frittata, melt the butter in a frying pan over medium heat. Carefully pour in the egg mixture. Continue cooking until the bottom is set and golden brown. Using a metal spatula, slip the frittata out onto a plate, right-side up. Return to the pan right-side down and cook for a few more minutes until set. If you like, cook the bottom of the frittata in the frying pan on the stove, then finish off under a hot grill, sprinkling the top with a little extra Parmesan before you do so. Be careful not to overcook – the egg continues cooking after you remove it from the heat. Leave in the pan until set firmly enough to slide out using a spatula. Serve warm or cold, cut into slices, accompanied by a fresh green salad or vegetable side dish.

Frittata di spinaci Blanch 10 ounces of spinach in boiling water for a couple of minutes until just wilted. (The length of time you need to do this depends on the age of the leaves; very young spinach leaves will wilt in hardly any time at all.) Drain well using a colander, then gently squeeze out any excess water from the spinach and chop finely. Heat 2 tablespoons of olive oil in a heavy frying pan over medium heat. Sauté the spinach for a minute or so until coated in the oil. Beat 5 large eggs with 2 tablespoons freshly grated Parmesan cheese. Season with salt and black pepper, then pour over the spinach. Mix gently, then continue cooking as for the potato frittata. SERVES 4

Frittata di cipolle Peel and finely slice 2¼ lb sweet onions. Soak in a bowl of cold water for 1 hour. Drain. Heat 2 tablespoons of olive oil in a heavy frying pan over medium heat. Sweat the onions for 20–30 minutes, stirring often, until soft and caramelized. Beat 10 large eggs with 3½ ounces of freshly grated Parmesan cheese. Season with salt and black pepper. When the onion is soft, pour the egg mixture over the top. Mix through gently, then continue cooking as for the potato frittata. SERVES 4

CONTORNI
Side dishes

FAGIOLINI INDORATI E FRITTI
Fried green beans

Choose the freshest beans you can find for this classic dish, typically sold in *friggitoria*, where the food goes literally straight from frying pan to table – or *frienn' magnann'*, as they say in the local dialect. The sweetness of the crisp beans contrasts perfectly with the Parmesan-flavored batter.

✣ SERVES 4

1 lb 2 oz fresh green beans, ends
  trimmed if necessary
light olive oil for shallow-frying
3 eggs
1³/4 oz Parmesan cheese, freshly grated
all-purpose flour for coating
salt

Blanch the beans in boiling salted water for a few minutes until just tender, but still with a bite. Drain, then put in a colander and rinse under cold running water to refresh (you want them to keep their bright-green color). Leave to cool while you prepare the coating.

Heat enough oil for shallow-frying in a heavy pan over medium heat. Beat the eggs with a little salt and the Parmesan cheese. When the oil is hot, quickly coat the beans in the flour and dip a few at a time into the egg mixture. Carefully drop them into the oil one by one, cooking in batches of three or four so that the temperature of the oil does not drop during cooking. Fry for a couple of minutes until golden, remove with a slotted spoon, and drain on paper towels. Repeat the process until all the beans have been used. Keep a production line going so that the beans are still crisp, piping hot, and at their best when they reach the table.

FAGIOLI IN UMIDO
Stewed beans in cherry tomato sauce

Fresh beans are best for this classic recipe, but you could use dried beans if fresh ones are not available. You will need to soak dried beans overnight in plenty of cold water with a pinch of baking soda, then rinse well before cooking. Variations of this dish are found throughout Italy – some are made with cannellini beans and sage; others use lentils.

✣ SERVES 4

3 tablespoons olive oil
2¹/4 lb fresh cannellini or borlotti
  beans, shelled
2 garlic cloves, finely chopped
1 celery stick, roughly chopped
1 fresh red chili, seeded and
  finely chopped
1³/4 oz fresh cherry tomatoes, cut
  into quarters
2 teaspoons dried oregano
salt and freshly ground black pepper

Heat 2 tablespoons of the oil in a heavy pan over medium heat. Add the beans, half the garlic, and the celery and sweat for a few minutes. Pour in just enough water to come about halfway up the beans, bring to a simmer, then cover the pan. Reduce the heat and simmer gently, stirring occasionally, for about 1 hour until the beans are tender but not mushy (adding extra water if necessary). Once they start to soften, season with salt and pepper. Just before the end of the cooking time, heat the remaining 1 tablespoon oil in a separate large pan over medium heat. Sweat the remaining garlic and the chili for a few minutes until soft and starting to color. Add the tomatoes and cook down for 5 minutes. Drain the beans and pick out and discard the celery. Add the beans to the tomato sauce. Check the seasoning, adding more salt if necessary, and sprinkle in the oregano. Stir through well and cook for another 5 minutes so that the flavors develop and meld. Serve immediately.

COFFEE CULTURE

Coffee is much more than a drink in Naples. In fact, drinking coffee is in many ways more of a pastime, and it is certainly steeped in ritual. If it is going to be proper coffee, most Neapolitans will tell you, it should be made from Arabica beans. Purists also say that to make a real cup of coffee at home you need a *caffettiera napoletana*, or Neapolitan drip-coffee pot. Traditionally made of metal, this is a nineteenth-century predecessor of the octagonal *moka* coffee pot. Like the *moka*, it comes in two parts, and is separated by a coffee filter. The bottom half is filled with water, then coffee grounds are lightly packed into the filter and the top replaced. The pot is put onto the heat to boil; as soon as the water starts to boil, the pot is removed from the heat and the coffee pot flipped upside down, allowing the water to filter slowly through the coffee. True aficionados will place a metal cover, a piece of foil, or a twist of newspaper – known as a *coppetiello* in the Neapolitan dialect – in the spout to keep the coffee hot and prevent the aromatic steam from escaping. Alfonso Bialetti's *moka caffettiera* is still commonly used, and those unwilling to wait for their coffee to drip through a *napoletana* always have at least one of these on hand.

Cafés and bars serving fine espresso coffee abound in Naples, and Neapolitans take the act of drinking a coffee at one of these establishments very seriously – in many cases they do so several times a day. It is this devotion to good coffee that has made Naples Italy's coffee-drinking capital. First, there is the question of what style of coffee to choose: a shot of *espresso*, a *caffè macchiato* (with a dash of milk), a *latte macchiato* (steamed milk with a dash of coffee, considered a breakfast drink or for those not up to drinking 'real' coffee), or a *cappuccino* (espresso with whipped steamed milk). Even here there are variations, as a *cappuccino* can come with froth or without, and be either cold, warm, or piping hot. Expert preparation of coffee is considered a fine art, and watching a white-jacketed Neapolitan barman preparing a cup leaves you with no doubt that this is absolutely true.

Neapolitans throng to the city's many coffee bars day and night, and everyone has their favorite. Still, it is hard to go past the Caffè Gambrinus, which has been serving coffee for 150 years and whose customers have included Guy de Maupassant and Oscar Wilde, without entering its ornate interior for a traditional cup.

INSALATA CAPRESE
Tomato, basil, and mozzarella salad

What could be more perfect on a summer day than this classic salad from the island of Capri, with its fabulous marriage of choice ingredients, fresh flavors, and aromas.

✤ SERVES 4

1 lb 2 oz flavorful ripe plum or round
  salad tomatoes, cut into slices
good-quality extra virgin olive oil
  for drizzling
1 lb 2 oz mozzarella cheese, cut into
  round slices
small handful of fresh oregano leaves
large bunch of fresh basil,
  leaves picked
salt and freshly ground black pepper

Layer the tomatoes on a platter or in a shallow serving dish. Season with salt and drizzle with a little oil. Arrange the slices of mozzarella over the slices of tomato. Sprinkle with the oregano and scatter over the basil leaves. Season well with black pepper and serve.

INSALATA DI FAGIOLI
White bean salad with tuna, spring onions, and olives

Another classic summertime dish, this simple Neapolitan salad once again makes the most of a few choice ingredients. This recipe combines elements of sea and land, with the saltiness of the tuna and olives providing a counterpoint to the sweet cannellini beans and tart dressing.

✤ SERVES 4

1 lb 2 oz fresh cannellini or borlotti
  beans, shelled
7-oz jar tuna in oil, drained
  and flaked
3 spring onions, green parts only,
  finely sliced on the diagonal
1³/₄ oz black olives, pitted
fresh flat-leaf parsley, leaves picked
  and chopped
1 tablespoon good-quality balsamic
  vinegar
2 tablespoons extra virgin olive oil
salt and freshly ground black pepper

Put the beans in a saucepan and cover with cold water. Bring to a boil and simmer gently for 15–20 minutes until tender but still whole. Drain and transfer to a serving bowl. Add the tuna, spring onions, and olives. Drizzle over the vinegar and oil, sprinkle in the parsley, and season with salt and black pepper. Toss gently but well. Cover and leave in the refrigerator for a couple of hours to allow the flavors to develop before serving.

CARCIOFI E PATATE
Braised artichokes and potatoes

Artichokes are a very popular vegetable in Campania and grow abundantly. Fresh or preserved, they are used throughout the year in dishes ranging from simple antipasti and soups, to pasta and side dishes. In this classic Neapolitan recipe, fresh artichokes are gently braised with potatoes, in the same delicious combination as in the potato and artichoke soup on page 28.

✢ SERVES 4

5 fresh artichokes
4 starchy potatoes, such as russet
4 tablespoons olive oil
generous handful of fresh flat-leaf
  parsley, or to taste, leaves picked
  and chopped
2 garlic cloves, peeled and
  lightly crushed
salt and freshly ground black pepper

Clean the artichokes well, removing the tough outer leaves. Using a teaspoon, remove and discard the central choke and any prickly inner leaves. Cut the artichokes into quarters. Peel the potatoes and cut into wedges. Heat the oil in a non-stick frying pan over medium heat and sweat the garlic for a few minutes until soft and golden. Remove the garlic from the pan using a slotted spoon and add the artichokes and potatoes. Quickly sweat in the pan for a few minutes until they are coated with the garlic-infused oil. Pour in enough water so that the vegetables are just covered. Let cook, with the pan half covered, for about 25 minutes. Make sure that the liquid has reduced completely before removing from the heat. Serve hot, sprinkled with parsley.

ZUCCHETTE E PATATE
Baby zucchini and potato stew

Zucchinis thrive in Campania's fertile soil and mild climate and are a staple of *cucina povera*, the cuisine which led to Neapolitans being known as *mangiafoglie* (leaf eaters). This particular recipe is traditionally served at Easter, along with several other signature dishes such as the more elaborate *minestra di Pasqua*, but works well at any time when baby zucchinis are in season.

✢ SERVES 4

1 lb 2 oz potatoes
2 teaspoons olive oil
1 onion, finely chopped
1 celery stick, chopped
3 lb 3 oz baby zucchinis, cut into
  largish pieces
salt and freshly ground black pepper
small handful of fresh flat-leaf
  parsley, leaves picked and chopped,
  to garnish

Peel the potatoes and cut into wedges. Heat a little olive oil in a pan over medium heat. Add the potatoes, onion, and celery and sweat until coated in oil. Pour in just enough water to come about halfway up the potatoes, bring to a simmer, and cover the pan. Reduce the heat, and continue cooking gently for 20 minutes, stirring occasionally, until the potatoes are nearly cooked. Add the zucchinis and continue cooking, covered, for another 5 minutes until the liquid has reduced and the vegetables are done – be careful not to let the zucchinis become too mushy. Season with salt and black pepper and scatter the parsley over the top. Serve hot.

ZUCCHINE UOVA E FORMAGGIO
Zucchinis with eggs, pancetta, and Parmesan

Many people think of zucchinis as being bland and watery, but the key is to choose zucchinis that are not too large and to combine them with other ingredients that enhance their flavor, as is the case in this simple yet delicious Easter recipe.

✧ SERVES 4

2 tablespoons olive oil
1 onion, finely chopped
1 3/4 oz pancetta, cut into 1/2-in cubes
2 1/4 lb zucchinis, cut into 1/2-in cubes
3 eggs
1–2 tablespoons freshly grated
  Parmesan cheese
handful of fresh flat-leaf parsley,
  leaves picked and chopped
salt and freshly ground black pepper

Heat the oil in a pan over medium heat. Sweat the onion and pancetta until the onion is soft and starting to caramelize. Add the zucchinis and season with salt and black pepper. Pour over 1 cup water, cover, and leave to cook gently for 15 minutes.

In the meantime, beat the eggs with a pinch of salt, the Parmesan, and the parsley. As soon as the zucchinis are cooked, add the beaten eggs and stir rapidly. Remove from the heat before the eggs are completely set and serve immediately

MELANZANE IN CARROZZA
Fried eggplant and provolone sandwiches

Hailing from the region around Mount Vesuvius, this recipe is another example of how to prepare food *in carrozza*, or "in a carriage" (see page 17). These eggplant sandwiches feature slices of *provola*, or provolone, a semi-hard cheese which is a speciality of Campania.

✧ SERVES 4

3 lb 3 oz eggplants
olive oil for shallow-frying
1 lb 2 oz unsmoked provolone cheese,
  cut into slices about 1/2-in thick
all-purpose flour for coating
5 eggs, beaten
salt and freshly ground black pepper

Cut the eggplants into round slices about ½ inch thick. Sprinkle with salt, place in a colander, put a weight on the top, and leave for about an hour to drain off any bitterness and excess liquid.

Rinse the eggplants well, pat dry with a clean towel or paper towels, and shallow-fry in very hot oil for about 5 minutes until they start to turn a golden color. Turn over and cook on the other side for a few more minutes. Drain on paper towels to remove any excess oil.

Place a slice of provola between 2 slices of the eggplant. Quickly coat with flour, dip in the beaten eggs, and shallow-fry in very hot oil until golden brown. Season with salt and black pepper and serve piping hot.

PARMIGIANA DI MELANZANE
Baked eggplants with tomatoes and mozzarella

Possibly one of Naples' best-known traditional dishes, and taken all over the world by the waves of migrants seeking a new life after World War II, *parmigiana di melanzane* is as tasty as it is familiar. Salting the eggplants before cooking is the key to success – otherwise you will end up with watery eggplants that fall apart when sliced. It is also important to press each layer down firmly when you are assembling the ingredients for baking.

✛ SERVES 4

2¹/₄ lb large eggplants
olive oil for cooking
1 garlic clove, finely chopped
2¹/₄ lb ripe tomatoes, preferably plum,
  peeled and chopped (see note)
10 oz mozzarella cheese
2–3 oz Parmesan cheese, grated
3 or 4 large fresh basil leaves,
  finely sliced
salt and freshly ground black pepper

Cut the eggplants into thick slices. Sprinkle with salt and leave in a colander, preferably overnight, to draw out the excess water. Rinse and pat dry with paper towels. Heat enough light olive oil for shallow-frying in a pan over medium-high heat and add the eggplant slices in a single layer. Shallow-fry on both sides for a few minutes until the slices start to brown slightly. Make sure that the oil is hot before adding the eggplants to the pan, so that they do not absorb too much oil. Remove from the pan with a slotted spoon and drain on paper towels.

Meanwhile, preheat the oven to 350°F (180°C). Make a tomato sauce by heating a little oil in a saucepan over medium heat. Add the garlic and cook until soft and transparent, before adding the tomatoes and basil. Season with salt and black pepper. Cook for 10 minutes until the tomatoes have broken up and reduced into a pulpy sauce.

As soon as the sauce is ready, arrange alternate layers of eggplant, tomato sauce, slices of mozzarella, and Parmesan in a greased baking dish. Make sure that you press down the ingredients well, so that you end up with compacted layers. Finish off with a layer of sauce and a sprinkling of Parmesan. Bake in the preheated oven for about 40 minutes. Let stand for a few minutes to allow the ingredients to set slightly, then cut into individual portions while still in the dish. Carefully slide out onto serving plates using a spatula, and serve hot.

Peeling tomatoes It is not such an onerous task, peeling fresh tomatoes. Simply score the skin slightly with a sharp knife, blanch in boiling water for 10 seconds or so until the skin starts to soften and split, then refresh in cold water. This makes it far easier to use a sharp knife to peel away the skin.

STUFATO DI VERDURE
Spicy ratatouille of peppers, eggplants, and potatoes

Not surprisingly for a traditional convent recipe, given these institutions' history of growing market produce, this dish draws heavily on the basic premise of using fresh produce to its best advantage – in this case, a heady and colorful mélange of vegetables.

✛ SERVES 4

2¼ lb red and yellow peppers
1 lb 10 oz starchy potatoes,
  such as russet
1¾ lb eggplants
2 tablespoons olive oil
2 garlic cloves
3 onions, chopped
7 oz ripe tomatoes, halved, seeded,
  and finely chopped
1 tablespoon finely chopped fresh
  oregano leaves or 2 teaspoons dried
2 or 3 large fresh basil leaves, or to
  taste, finely sliced
salt and freshly ground black pepper

Remove the stalk, seeds, and membrane from the peppers, and cut into thin strips. Peel the potatoes and cut into ½ inch cubes. Dice the eggplants into a similar size.

Heat the oil in a pan over medium heat and sweat the onions and garlic for a few minutes until soft. Add the tomatoes and allow to cook down slightly, then add the peppers, eggplants, and potatoes. Stir through to coat the vegetables in the oil, then season with salt, cover the pan, and cook over medium heat for about 30 minutes.

Remove the lid from the pan and cook the vegetable mixture for a few more minutes to allow the liquid to reduce. Sprinkle over the oregano and basil (if using dried oregano, you may wish to add it a little earlier while you are reducing the liquid, so that the flavor develops). Serve hot or cold.

CARCIOFI INDORATI E FRITTI
Deep-fried artichokes

Deep-fried artichokes are often served in Naples' *trattorie* and are just one of the array of *frienn' magnann'* (fry and eat) delicacies that are so much a part of the city's street and food life.

✛ SERVES 4

8 artichokes
juice of 1 lemon, to acidulate
  artichokes
3 eggs
2 oz Parmesan cheese, grated
pinch of salt
3½ oz all-purpose or tipo 00 flour
light olive oil for deep-frying
sea salt, to serve

Remove the tough outer leaves from the artichokes. Snip the tops off the larger leaves. Let soak for 30 minutes in a bowl of water with the lemon juice. Using a teaspoon, remove the choke and any prickly inner leaves. Cut each artichoke into 4 wedges.

To make the batter for coating the artichokes, beat the eggs with the Parmesan and salt. Coat the artichoke pieces in the flour, gently shake off any excess, then dip in the beaten egg. Deep-fry in batches in very hot oil for 5–10 minutes until golden brown, depending on the size of the artichokes. Remove with a slotted spoon and drain on paper towels. Serve piping hot, with a bowl of sea salt at the table for seasoning.

ZUCCHINE CON LA MOZZARELLA
Baked zucchinis and mozzarella

Traditionally served at Easter, this dish is a fine example of layering and baking vegetables to bring out their flavor. This technique is a feature of Campanian cuisine, and conforms to the tenets of slow cooking found throughout the region, and particularly in the revered *ragù*. Usually this type of dish would be made in a special clay pot, but a good ceramic baking dish will suffice.

✣ SERVES 4

2 tablespoons olive oil
2$\frac{1}{4}$ lb zucchinis, cut into rounds
10 oz buffalo mozzarella, cut
 into slices
1–2 tablespoons freshly grated
 Parmesan cheese
2 or 3 large fresh basil leaves, torn
 into small pieces
1$\frac{3}{4}$ oz butter
salt and freshly ground black pepper

Preheat the oven to 300°F (150°C). Heat the olive oil in a heavy pan over medium heat. Add the zucchinis and sauté for 5–10 minutes until they start to brown. Remove from the pan with a slotted spoon and drain briefly on paper towels.

Arrange a layer of zucchinis in the bottom of a baking dish. Cover with a layer of mozzarella, sprinkle with some Parmesan and basil, and season with salt and black pepper. Repeat the process, finishing off with a layer of zucchinis. Cover with grated Parmesan and dot with the butter. Bake in the preheated oven for 15 minutes and serve immediately.

PEPERONI IMBOTTITE
Roasted peppers stuffed with eggplant, olives, and capers

These exquisite stuffed peppers come from the volcanic island of Ischia, at the northern end of the Gulf of Naples. The peppers are chargrilled first, then their skins peeled and the insides removed. This enhances their sweetness, so that they almost melt in your mouth and contrast beautifully with the textures and flavors of the piquant stuffing. *Peperoni imbottite* certainly deserve their place in the line-up of dishes that typify the cuisine of Naples and its surroundings. You can easily increase the quantities to make a larger amount.

✢ SERVES 4–6

6 red peppers
1 lb 2 oz eggplants, cut into
  1/2-in cubes
olive oil for cooking
6 slices of good-quality stale bread
  such as ciabatta or pane casereccio,
  cut into 1/2-in cubes
3 oz olives, pitted and halved
2 1/2 oz salted capers, rinsed and
  squeezed dry
2 garlic cloves, finely chopped
2 salted anchovy filets, chopped
handful of fresh flat-leaf parsley,
  leaves picked and chopped
salt and freshly ground black pepper

Preheat the oven to 300 (150°C). Char the peppers over an open flame or under a hot grill until their skins are blistered and blackened in places. Carefully peel off the skin and discard. (Use rubber gloves if the peppers are too hot to handle, and you can also put them in a plastic bag for a few minutes after charring, to help make the skins easier to remove.) Carefully remove and discard the stem, central membrane, and seeds, taking care to keep the peppers whole.

Heat a little olive oil in a frying pan over medium heat. Add the eggplants and sauté for a few minutes until they start to brown. Remove from the pan with a slotted spoon, and drain on paper towels while you cook the bread. Using the same pan, gently fry the bread cubes until golden, adding a little extra oil if necessary.

Remove the croutons from the pan and carefully mix with the eggplants, olives, capers, garlic, anchovies, and parsley to make a stuffing. Season with salt and black pepper. Using a spoon, fill the peppers with the stuffing until they are nice and plump and the stuffing is slightly mounded at the top. Arrange in a baking tin or dish, drizzle with extra olive oil, and roast in the preheated oven for 20–25 minutes. Serve hot or cold.

PIZZA E PANE

Pizza and bread

WOOD-FIRED PIZZA

There is no doubt that Naples is the true home of pizza –
all you need to do is ask a Neapolitan. Pizza has traveled
around the world and is now served in all sorts of
variations, but its roots lie in very humble beginnings – that
of the poor people who flocked to Naples in the early
eighteenth century, looking for work and a place to live.
Necessity is the mother of invention, and the pizza was
originally little more than a dough of flour, water, and salt,
with a simple tomato topping. Although tomatoes had been
brought back to Europe by the Portuguese after their travels
to South America, they were long regarded as poisonous
and only used as ornamental plants. It was not until the
eighteenth century, particularly around Naples and Salerno,
that they were cultivated for food.

It was not long before pizza had become a staple among
the poor of Naples, and *pizzaioli* (pizza-makers) were selling
their wares on the street, drawing visitors from outside into
the poor areas to sample the dish. Officially, Naples' first
pizzeria (pizzas were initially sold by people walking up and
down the street touting freshly made pizza from nearby
pizzaiolo kitchens), the Port 'Alba, opened in 1830; it still
runs today and revels in its claim to being the first. The first
pizza topping was marinara. Despite the name, it contains
no seafood, but instead is named for its popularity with the
hungry fishermen who would devour this dish at the end of

a long night hauling in fish. It is made with a tomato,
garlic, and oregano.

Before long, the nobility and even the royal household
became enamored, and the pizza became firmly implanted
in Neapolitan cuisine. In 1889, Raffaele Esposito of the
pizzeria Brandi (also still open today) invented the pizza
Margherita, named in honor of the wife of King of Italy
Umberto I. It is from these two original authentic toppings
that all subsequent pizzas have come. By the end of the
nineteenth century, pizza could be eaten at any time of the
day, bought from one of the many stalls and pizzerias built
to cater to the seemingly incessant demand.

Neapolitans are so proud of the pizza – and certain
devotees so determined to maintain its integrity – that there
is even an organization dedicated to ensuring that it is made
to the correct standards using traditional methods: the
Associazione Vera Pizza Napoletana. Rules for an authentic
pizza are: the dough must be made of flour, natural or
brewer's yeast, salt, and water only; the dough must be
kneaded by hand (or only by devices approved by the
association); the pizza must be cooked directly on the oven
floor; and it must be baked in a traditional bell-shaped
wood-fired oven. There are more than 500 pizzerias in
Naples: Port 'Alba, Brandi, Cafasso, da Michele, di Matteo,
da Pasqualino, Trianon ... the list goes on ... and on.

PASTA PER PIZZE
Basic pizza dough

Making your own pizza dough is truly a simple task, and it provides you with a pizza base far superior to any shop-bought version. Kneading dough is so therapeutic, you should be in exactly the right frame of mind to devour your pizza when it is ready.

✣ MAKES ENOUGH FOR 4 LARGE PIZZAS

1 oz fresh yeast
2 cups warm water
$2^1/_4$ lb all-purpose flour or tipo 0 flour
pinch of salt

Dissolve the yeast in a little of the warm water. Sprinkle in a handful of the flour and mix well. Shape into a small ball and leave to rise in a dry place for 30 minutes. Make a well in the center of the flour and add the yeast mixture, remaining warm water, and a pinch of salt. Knead vigorously on a floured work surface for about 10 minutes, adding some warm water a little at a time until the dough is smooth but not sticky. Place on an oiled baking sheet and flatten out the dough with your hands, then cover with the topping of your choice. (You can freeze this dough to use later, but it is at its best when fresh.)

Pizza marinara This is the original and some would say the best, the roots from which all subsequent pizzas have sprung. To make 2 large pizzas, take ½ quantity of basic dough; shape into rounds. Using your knuckles, lightly press down around the edge of the dough about $1^1/_4$ inches in from the edge, to make a slight rim. Drain 14 ounces cannned peeled plum tomatoes in a colander, pressing down gently to remove any excess juice. Roughly chop, then spread the tomato evenly over the dough, leaving a border of about 1 inch. Sprinkle over 2–3 thinly sliced garlic cloves and 2–3 teaspoons dried oregano. Drizzle generously with 3 tablespoons or so of olive oil. Season with salt and freshly ground black pepper. Slide onto an unglazed terracotta tile, pizza stone, pizza pan, or baking sheet, and bake in the center of a preheated oven at 450°–475° (230°–240°C) for 8–10 minutes until crisp.

Pizza Margherita To make 2 large pizzas, take ½ quantity of basic dough and prepare as for pizza marinara. Drain 14 ounces canned peeled plum tomatoes in a colander, pressing down gently to remove any excess juice. Roughly chop, then spread the tomato evenly over the dough, leaving a border of about 1 inch. Season with salt and drizzle generously with 2–3 tablespoons olive oil. Spread over 5 ounces halved cherry tomatoes and 5–7 ounces drained sliced mozzarella cheese. Scatter over 10–12 finely sliced large fresh basil leaves. Sprinkle with a little grated Parmesan, to taste. Slide onto an unglazed terracotta tile, pizza stone, pizza pan, or baking sheet, and bake in the center of a preheated oven at 450°–475° (230°–240°C) for 8–10 minutes until crisp.

CALZONE DI RICOTTA E SALAME
Ricotta and salami calzone

Calzone usually contains a filling based on a mixture of ricotta and mozzarella cheese. It makes for perfect street food, and in Naples, kiosks and *trattorie* do a brisk business with this treat.

⊹ SERVES 4–6

1/2 quantity of basic pizza dough
  (see page 129)
7 oz fresh ricotta, drained
2 tablespoons freshly grated
  Parmesan cheese
3¹/2 oz buffalo mozzarella cheese,
  diced
3¹/2 oz spicy salami such as napoli or
  milano, diced
3 or 4 large fresh basil leaves, torn
extra virgin olive oil for drizzling
freshly ground black pepper

Preheat the oven to 450°–475° (230°–240°C). Prepare the basic pizza dough as on page 129. Put the ricotta, Parmesan, mozzarella, and salami in a bowl. Sprinkle in the basil and season with black pepper. Mix until smooth and well combined. On a floured work surface, form the dough into a large round, and put the filling in a mound in the center of the dough. Fold over in half to form a half-moon parcel. Press the edges together well so that the calzone is sealed tightly and the filling will not ooze out. Transfer to an oiled baking sheet, and drizzle a little oil over the calzone. Bake in the center of the preheated oven for 8–12 minutes until crisp and golden.

Pizza fritta A Neapolitan speciality with a long tradition, *pizza fritta* is similar to calzone in that it is filled and the dough folded over on itself to form a parcel. The difference comes in the cooking. Instead of being baked, it is deep-fried in very hot oil or lard – definitely reserved for the very hungry.

PIZZA CON SALSICCIA PICCANTE E PATATE
Spicy sausage and potato pizza

This hearty and flavorful pizza is based on the principle of using few but quality ingredients.

⊹ MAKES 2 LARGE PIZZAS OR
4 INDIVIDUAL ONES

1/2 quantity of basic pizza dough
  (see page 129)
5 oz buffalo mozzarella cheese, sliced
10 oz ripe cherry tomatoes, halved, or
  plum tomatoes, sliced
3¹/2 oz new potatoes, sliced
3¹/2–5 oz spicy Italian sausage, such
  as salami napoli, sliced
3 or 4 teaspoons fresh rosemary
  leaves, chopped
2 tablespoons extra virgin olive oil
sea salt

Prepare the pizza dough as on page 129. Flatten out with your hands into 2 large rounds, or divide the dough into 4 and make individual rounds. Using your knuckles, lightly press down around the edge of the dough about 1 inch in from the edge, to make a slight rim. Top with the mozzarella slices. Spread around the cherry tomatoes, potato slices, and spicy sausage. Sprinkle over the rosemary and season with sea salt. Drizzle the pizza with a little olive oil. Slide the pizza onto an unglazed tile, pizza stone, oiled pizza pan, or oiled baking sheet. Bake in the center of a preheated oven at 450°–475°F (230°–240°C) for 8–12 minutes until the base is crisp.

PIZZA CAPPERI, OLIVE E ACCIUGHE
Pizza with capers, olives, and anchovies

Capers, olives, and anchovies are three signature ingredients of Campanian cuisine, and of the cuisines of Southern Italy in general. They work well in combination, as seen in this classic pizza topping, with their strong, salty flavors cutting through the richness of the mozzarella and sweet tang of the cherry tomatoes.

✤ MAKES 2 LARGE PIZZAS OR
4 INDIVIDUAL ONES

¹/₂ quantity of basic pizza dough
  (see page 129)
10 oz ripe cherry tomatoes, halved
5 oz mozzarella cheese, sliced
25–30 anchovy filets in olive oil,
  drained
4 tablespoons salted capers, rinsed
  and gently squeezed dry
  (you can be more generous with
  these if you like)
12–15 black olives, such as Gaeta,
  pitted and chopped
2–3 teaspoons dried oregano
2–3 teaspoons extra virgin olive oil

Prepare the pizza dough as on page 129. Flatten out with your hands into 2 large rounds, or divide the dough into 4 and make individual rounds. Using your knuckles, lightly press down around the edge of the dough about 1 inch in from the edge, to make a slight rim. Spread the tomatoes over the base of the pizza, leaving a border at the edge. Lay the anchovy filets on top, spreading them around the base evenly. Sprinkle on the capers and olives, and scatter the oregano over the top. Drizzle the pizza with a little extra virgin olive oil (or you could use the drained oil from the anchovies if you like). Slide the pizza onto an unglazed tile, pizza stone, pizza pan, or baking sheet, and bake in the center of a preheated oven at 450°–475°F (230°–240°C) for 8–12 minutes until the base is crisp.

IMPASTO PER PANE
Basic bread dough

The smell of baking bread is evocative of warmth and home. You can use this basic bread dough to make a rustic, country-style loaf or as the basis for breads such as the rosemary loaf below. Although similar to the classic sourdough *pane casereccio*, it is made without the *biga*, or starter, that is so much a part of the latter. Starters are an important part of Italian bread making; in some households the *biga* is kept going for years, ready to be used as the base of delicious homemade bread. With this recipe, though, you can make your own fresh crusty bread with relative ease.

✢ MAKES 1 LARGE LOAF

$1^3/_4$ oz fresh yeast
$1^3/_4$ cups warm water
1 lb 2 oz plus $1^1/_2$ tablespoons
  all-purpose or tipo 0 flour
2 teaspoons salt

Crumble the yeast into a bowl and dissolve in $3/_4$ cup of the warm water. Add the $1^1/_2$ tablespoons of flour, mix together, and shape into a soft round ball. Leave to rise in a warm place until it has doubled in size.

Make a well in the center of the 1 lb 2 ounces flour and add the salt. Add enough of the remaining warm water, a little at a time, to make a soft but not sticky dough. Add the yeast mixture and knead vigorously for about 20 minutes until the dough is soft and springy. Shape the dough into a ball, place in an oiled or buttered bowl, and make a cross-shaped cut in the top. Cover with a floured dish towel. Leave to rise at about 80°F (28°C) in a draft-free place to prevent the top from drying out and forming a crust.

When the dough has doubled in size and leaves a dimple when you press lightly with your finger, knead again for a few minutes. Divide into portions, and shape as you wish. Bake on a lightly greased and floured baking sheet in a preheated oven at 475°F (240°C) for 40 minutes or until golden brown. The loaf should sound hollow when tapped on the bottom.

PANE AL ROSMARINO
Rosemary bread

Gently infusing the oil used in this bread with fresh rosemary means that the herb's distinctive flavor permeates the bread without being overpowering. You could experiment with fresh thyme instead, or other flavorings such as fennel seed, if you wish.

✢ MAKES 4 SMALL LOAVES

1 quantity of basic bread dough
  (see above)
$1/_4$ cup olive oil
2 or 3 sprigs (4-in stem) fresh
  rosemary
pinch of salt

Prepare the dough as above. Heat the oil in a small frying pan over gentle heat. Add the rosemary, reserving 10 leaves. Soften over gentle heat for 5 minutes, remove the sprigs and allow the oil to cool. Finely chop the reserved rosemary leaves. Add the rosemary-infused oil, chopped rosemary, and a pinch of salt to the dough and knead well. Divide the dough into 4 small rounds and let rise in a warm place for about 30 minutes. To bake, make a cross-shaped cut on the top of each loaf, then brush with some of the leftover rosemary-infused oil. Bake in a preheated oven at 475°F (240°C) for 40 minutes or until golden brown. Remove from the oven and serve.

PANE DI OLIVE
Olive bread

Do not skimp on the olives you use in this delicious chewy bread, and avoid those that are sold already pitted – they are usually of inferior quality. Just keep in mind the cornerstone of this regional cuisine: select the finest produce you can find for simple but stunning results.

✢ MAKES 1 LOAF

1 lb 2 oz all-purpose or tipo 0 flour
pinch of salt
1 oz fresh yeast
1 cup warm water
3^1/$_2$ oz butter, melted
5 oz black olives such as Gaeta,
  pitted and halved

In a large bowl, mix the flour with a pinch of salt and make a well in the center. Crumble the yeast into a small bowl and dissolve in the warm water. Add the yeast liquid and combine well, adding a little more warm water if necessary. Transfer the dough to a floured work surface and knead for about 10 minutes until the dough is firm and springy, working in the butter as you go. Shape into a ball, place in an oiled bowl, and cover with a clean dish towel. Leave to rise for about 1 hour in a warm place.

When the dough has risen, knead again briefly and add the olives, mixing in well. Shape into a ball, replace in the oiled bowl, and leave to rise once more, covered with a dish towel, for about 1^1/$_2$ hours or until cracks start to appear on the surface. Grease a baking sheet and flour lightly. Place the dough on the baking sheet and bake in a preheated oven at 475°F (240°C) for about 40 minutes or until the top is golden and the bread sounds hollow when knocked on the bottom. Remove from the oven and serve.

PANE DI NOCE
Walnut bread

Walnuts have grown in Campania for centuries, and from their original habitat on the Sorrento Peninsula they have spread throughout the region. They are now widely cultivated in the ideal rich volcanic soil of the area, cementing their place in both Campania's agriculture and its cuisine.

✢ MAKES 1 LOAF

1 lb 2 oz all-purpose or tipo 0 flour
3^1/$_2$ oz whole-wheat flour
pinch of salt
1 oz fresh yeast
^{2}/$_3$ cup warm milk
3^1/$_2$ oz butter, melted
3^1/$_2$ oz walnuts, freshly chopped
1^3/$_4$ oz pine nuts

Mix together the two types of flour with a pinch of salt, and make a well in the center. Dissolve the yeast in the warm milk. Add to the flour with the melted butter. Knead well for 10 minutes until the dough is soft and springy, adding a little warm water if necessary. Add two-thirds of the walnuts and pine nuts, mixing in well. Shape the dough into a ball and put in a large oiled bowl. Cover with a clean dish towel and let rise in a warm place for about 45 minutes.

When the dough has risen, knead once again, then shape into a round loaf and place on a greased and lightly floured baking sheet. Flatten out the dough slightly with your hands and let rise for another 45 minutes. Brush the dough with a little water and sprinkle over the remaining walnuts and pine nuts. Bake in a preheated oven at 475°F (240°C) for about 40 minutes or until the crust is golden. Remove from the oven and serve.

DOLCI
Desserts and pastries

PASTIERA NAPOLETANA
Neapolitan wheat-grain and ricotta Easter tart

Neapolitan cuisine is peppered with dishes that are strongly associated with particular festivals and celebrations, or particular times of the year. *Pastiera napoletana* is one such dish, and is traditionally served at Easter. Although now associated with the Christian calendar, its roots are thought to be much older than this – indeed, centuries old – and lie in the pagan ritual of making offerings to the arrival of spring. Lard is traditionally used for the pastry, which makes it very short and light, but you can use butter or white vegetable shortening, if you prefer.

✥ SERVES 6–8

7 oz wheat grain (with the husks removed)

6 cups milk

grated zest of $^1/_2$ lemon

1–2 teaspoons ground cinnamon

1 teaspoon pure vanilla extract

grated zest of $^1/_2$ orange

10 oz tipo 00 flour or all-purpose flour

14 oz sugar

5 oz lard or butter, or half and half of each

4 large eggs, separated, plus 3 extra yolks

10 oz ricotta

7 oz candied citrus peel, chopped

2 tablespoons orange-flower water (available in gourmet food shops)

salt

confectioners' sugar for dusting

Soak the grain in plenty of cold water for a few days, changing the water every day. Some recipes actually call for the wheat to be soaked for a period of 2 weeks before being used – but just long enough to soften the grain and allow it to expand is enough. (Alternatively, you can use ready-to-use precooked wheat, which is available in cans from good Italian delicatessens.) Drain and simmer gently in the milk over very low heat, covered, for about 4 hours with the grated zest of $^1/_2$ lemon and a pinch of salt. Remove from the heat and drain off any excess liquid, then flavor the grain with the cinnamon, vanilla, and the grated zest of $^1/_2$ orange. Leave in the refrigerator overnight to allow the flavor to develop.

Make the shortcrust pastry. Sift the flour and a pinch of salt into a bowl. Add 5 ounces of the sugar and rub in the lard or butter with your fingertips until the mixture resembles rough breadcrumbs. Make a well in the center and add 3 egg yolks. Draw together into a dough, form into a flattish disc, wrap in cling wrap, and let sit in the refrigerator for 2 hours.

In the meantime, preheat the oven to 300°F (150°C). Mix the ricotta in a bowl with the remaining 9 ounces of sugar, 4 egg yolks, the candied peel, orange-flower water, and 4 beaten egg whites. Roll out the pastry and use to line a greased round pie plate about 12 inches in diameter and 3 inches deep, keeping a little pastry aside for decoration. Add the soaked grain to the ricotta and fold in delicately. Pour into the pastry case. Roll out the remaining pastry into strips (you may need to add a little extra flour, as the pastry is so short – this will make it easier to work with), and place over the filling in a diamond lattice pattern. Bake in the oven for about 40 minutes or until set and the pastry is golden. Allow to cool, and dust with confectioners' sugar before serving.

CREMA DI CIOCCOLATA
Chocolate cream with citron and orange peel

Carnevale is a celebration that culminates in Mardi Gras ("Fat Tuesday" or Shrove Tuesday). Mardi Gras is seen as one last day of parades and gaiety before Lent. This traditional carnival dessert was formerly made with pig's blood, known as *sanguinaccio*. The Neapolitan version is a rich thick cream usually eaten cold with *savoiardi* biscuits. This is a chocolate-only recipe.

⊹ SERVES 4

3¹/₂ oz plain cocoa powder
1 lb superfine sugar
4 teaspoons Italian tipo 00 flour or
  plain flour
2 teaspoons corn flour
1 cup milk
1 tablespoon butter
1 tablespoon pure vanilla extract
1 tablespoon ground cinnamon
1³/₄ oz candied citrus peel
savoiardi (Italian sponge fingers),
  to serve

In a saucepan, thoroughly mix the cocoa powder, sugar, flour, corn flour, milk, butter, half the vanilla extract, and the cinnamon. Cook over gentle heat until the mixture comes to a boil, stirring constantly. Remove from the heat and add the citrus peel and the remaining vanilla. Stir through, then leave to set before serving – the consistency should not be too thick. Serve with *savoiardi* for dipping into the chocolate cream.

Note If you are a real chocoholic, you can add some good-quality grated dark chocolate (at least 70% cocoa solids) to the cream at the same time as the peel, and stir through to melt – this makes the dessert sinfully rich, which seems appropriate given *sanguinaccio's* association with *Carnevale* and the period preceding Lent.

BISCOTTI AL CIOCCOLATO E MANDORLE
Chocolate and almond biscuits

These biscuits are from an old beloved family recipe. The mixture is rolled out like pastry and cut into any shape you prefer. Almonds grow prolifically in Campania and are an important agricultural crop, turning up in everything from sweets such as sugared almonds (known as *confetti* in Italy) and *torrone* (nougat), to wine and liqueurs.

⊹ SERVES 4

10 oz Italian tipo 00 flour or
  all-purpose flour
3¹/₂ oz plain cocoa powder
5 oz sugar
1 tablespoon baking powder
1 large egg plus 2 large egg yolks
3¹/₂ oz almonds, blanched
  and chopped

Preheat the oven to 350°F (180°C). Put the flour in a bowl and make a well in the center. Add the remaining ingredients and beat vigorously until smooth (if the mixture is not coming together, you may need to add another egg, but do not make it too wet).

Roll out the mixture to a thickness of ¹/₄ inch and cut into shapes using a pastry cutter, or even a glass turned upside down. Arrange on a greased baking sheet and bake in the oven for 30 minutes until crisp. Cool on a wire rack before eating. These biscuits will keep for up to a week if stored in an airtight container.

BISCOTTI ROCCOCÒ
Almond Christmas biscuits

Roccocò are a speciality of Campania and are typically served as a dessert at Christmas time, but they make an excellent treat at any time of the year. Redolent with spices and citrus, and made in a traditional ring, or doughnut, shape, these crisp biscuits echo the Arab influence on the region, and indeed much of Southern Italy.

✢ MAKES ABOUT 20

5 oz sweet almonds
10 oz Italian tipo 00 flour
10 oz sugar
1 tablespoon ammonium bicarbonate
 (see note)
grated zest of 1 lemon
grated zest of 1 orange
pinch of freshly grated nutmeg
1 teaspoon ground cinnamon
1/2 cup sweet white wine or water
41/2 oz candied citrus peel, finely
 chopped
1 large egg, beaten
confectioners' sugar for dusting

Preheat the oven to 350°F (180°C). Blanch the almonds in very hot water for 5 minutes. Peel and arrange in a single layer on a baking sheet. Leave the almonds in the warm oven for a few minutes to dry out, then roughly chop.

On a pastry board, mix the flour with the sugar, almonds, ammonium bicarbonate, lemon and orange zest, nutmeg, and cinnamon. Add just enough of the wine or water, a little at a time, to form a stiff dough. Next, mix in the candied citrus peel, and form the dough into 20 balls. Shape each ball of dough into a sausage shape about 6 inches long, overlap the ends slightly, and join to form flattish rings like doughnuts.

Lightly grease a baking sheet and arrange the rings in rows. Brush the tops with the beaten egg to glaze, and bake in the oven for about 25 minutes or until golden. Cool a little, dust liberally with confectioners' sugar, and serve.

Note The ammonium bicarbonate traditionally used to make these biscuits can be substituted with 1/2 tablespoon baking powder and 1/2 tablespoon baking soda.

TORTA CAPRESE
Chocolate almond cake

The island of Capri is a gem, and so is this moist textured cake with chocolate and almonds. Capri is famed for its limoncello, and this liqueur gives this cake its distinctive citrus twist. Examples of this cake can be found in bakeries and *pasticcerie* throughout Campania.

⁜ SERVES 6–8

9 oz butter

6 eggs, separated

9 oz sugar

1/4 cup citrus liqueur, preferably limoncello

14 oz blanched almonds, roughly chopped

9 oz good-quality dark chocolate, roughly chopped

confectioners' sugar for dusting

Preheat the oven to 350°C (180°C). Melt the butter in a double boiler, then allow to cool slightly. In a large bowl, beat the egg yolks with the sugar and liqueur until creamy. Whip the egg whites and fold into the egg yolk mixture with the butter. Sprinkle in the almonds and chocolate and fold gently through the mixture. (If the mixture is too runny, add a few more chopped almonds.)

Line a large round cake tin with parchment paper and pour in the mixture. Bake in the preheated oven for about an hour or until a skewer inserted into the center of the cake comes out clean. Allow to cool slightly, then dust generously with confectioners' sugar and serve.

Note In this recipe, the almonds and eggs give the cake its body. If you would prefer a smoother texture, simply chop the almonds more finely and grate the chocolate before adding to the mixture. This is how you would usually find it prepared if you bought it from a Campanian bakery.

SFOGLIATELLE RICCE
Semolina and ricotta pastries

Sfogliatelle have a long history that began in the 1700s in the kitchens of the Croce di Lucca monastery, where *sfogliatelle ricce* were prepared for visitors. A later version was made by the cloistered nuns at the Santa Rosa convent on the Amalfi coast. It was in 1818 that *sfogliatelle* were first produced outside the monastery and convent kitchens by Pasquale Pintauro, a baker on Naples' via Toledo, who served them in a seemingly never-ending stream to his customers (the Pintauro bakery still exists today). Soon bakeries and *pasticcerie* all over Naples were imitating him. Today, *sfogliatelle* are considered the queen of Neapolitan pastries. *Sfogliatelle ricce* have a characteristic clam shape and flaky pastry. *Sfogliatelle frolle* are shaped more like an oval bun and are made of a smooth shortcrust pastry. *Sfogliatelle Santa Rosa* have a rich custard cream and black cherry filling; made of the same pastry, they are larger and folded like a turnover.

✣ SERVES 4

For the pastry
12 oz Italian tipo 00 flour or
  all-purpose flour
pinch of salt
6 oz lard or butter, or half and half of
  each, softened and cut into chunks,
  plus extra, melted, for brushing

For the filling
5 oz semolina
7 oz ricotta
5 oz confectioners' sugar
1 tablespoon pure vanilla extract
1 large egg, beaten
3 oz candied citrus peel, finely
  chopped
pinch of ground cinnamon
confectioners' sugar for dusting

Sift the flour into a large bowl with a pinch of salt. Make a well in the center. Rub in the butter with your fingertips, then add $1/2$ cup water and mix to form a dough. Knead for several minutes until smooth. Shape into a ball, wrap in cling wrap, and chill for 2–3 hours.

On a floured work surface, roll out the dough very thinly into a rectangle about 28 x 24 inches. Trim the edges. Cut into four equal pieces lengthwise, so that you have four strips, each about 28 x 6 inches. Brush the melted lard or butter over a strip evenly and generously. Carefully lift the second strip of pastry and place it over the first. Brush generously and evenly with the lard or butter. Repeat with the remaining strips, so that each one is separated by a layer of shortening. Allow to set. Gently roll up from one short end like a Swiss roll, wrap in cling wrap and chill for 2–3 hours.

Bring $1^2/3$ cups water to a boil in a saucepan with a pinch of salt. Sprinkle in the semolina and cook for about 5 minutes, stirring all the time with a wooden spoon. Leave to sit in the refrigerator for 2–3 hours.

Preheat the oven to 400°F (200°C). Pass the ricotta through a sieve and add the confectioners' sugar, vanilla, egg, candied peel, cinnamon, and cooked semolina. Mix thoroughly and set aside.

Trim the ends of the pastry evenly using a small sharp knife. Cut the roll into 12 discs about $1/2$ inch thick. Sprinkle lightly with flour, then gently roll out each disc in four directions from the center so that you have slightly oval shapes. Pick up a pastry oval in the palm of your hand, rolled side down, and cup your hand slightly. Push down gently in the center of the pastry so that you form a cone. Put some filling in the pocket, then lightly squeeze to form a clam shape. Press down tightly to seal the edges and pinch the narrow end slightly to accentuate the clam shape. Repeat with the remaining pastry. Brush with extra melted lard or butter. Bake in the oven on a greased baking sheet for 20–25 minutes until golden, brushing with melted lard or butter once or twice as they cook. Serve warm, dusted with confectioners' sugar.

ZEPPOLE DI SAN GIUSEPPE
Deep-fried pastry puffs

Traditionally made to celebrate the Feast of Saint Joseph on March 19th, which is observed throughout Italy, these pastries, or at least the consuming of them, are a time-honored ritual in Naples. Eating *zeppole* on St. Joseph's Day is as ingrained a custom as the traditional wearing of red clothing, the outdoor market on via Guglielmo Sanfelice, and via Medina selling caged birds and toys to excited children. *Pasticcerie* and *friggitorie* (shops selling fried food) all over the city serve them by the dozen, piping hot, to lines of hungry customers.

✣ SERVES 4

9 oz butter
pinch of salt
14 oz Italian tipo 00 flour or
  all-purpose flour
12 large egg yolks
3 large egg whites
vegetable oil for deep-frying
confectioners' sugar for dusting
2 cups milk
7 oz sugar
1 tablespoon pure vanilla extract
9 oz black cherry jam, to decorate

Put 2 cups water, butter, and a pinch of salt into a pan and bring to a boil. Remove from the heat and sprinkle in the flour, stirring continuously until the mixture comes away from the sides of the pan. Allow to cool a little, then beat in 9 of the egg yolks and the 3 egg whites using a wooden spoon. Transfer the mixture to a pastry bag and, using a large piping nozzle, pipe small ring-shaped doughnuts onto wax paper or similar.

Heat enough oil for deep-frying in a heavy deep-sided saucepan over medium-high heat. To test whether the oil is hot enough, carefully slide one of the pastries into the pan using a metal spatula – it should sizzle right away. Cooking in batches, deep-fry the pastries for 5 minutes, until golden. Remove from the oil using a slotted spoon and drain on paper towels. Cool slightly, then dust liberally with confectioners' sugar.

Meanwhile, to make the *crema pasticciera* (custard cream), combine the milk, sugar, the remaining 3 egg yolks, and the vanilla in a small saucepan. Bring to a boil over gentle heat, stirring until thickened. Use to decorate the *zeppole*, piping a little custard cream into the center of each one. Dot a teaspoonful of black cherry jam on top of the custard cream, and serve the *zeppole* warm or cold.

FRITTELLE
Sweet potato fritters

A *cucina povera* recipe, these crisp, sweet fritters are typical of the *passatèmpi* or *merende* (snacks) sold on the street stalls and kiosks all around Naples. They are at their best and most irresistible when served freshly made and piping hot – *frienn' magnann'*.

✢ SERVES 4

14 oz starchy potatoes, such as russet
1 lb Italian tipo 00 flour or
  all-purpose flour
³/₄ oz fresh yeast
a little milk
1 tablespoon sugar
³/₄ cup vegetable oil plus extra for
  deep-frying
2 large eggs
grated zest of 1 lemon
superfine sugar for sprinkling

Boil, peel, and mash the potatoes. Make a well in the flour and add the yeast, a little milk, and all the other ingredients. Knead vigorously for 15 minutes. Break off into about 40 equal-sized balls, each the size of a tablespoon. Roll out into sausage-like strips and join the ends together, overlapping them slightly and pinching gently together to form rings. Lay out on a greased baking sheet, cover with a clean dish towel, and let rise for about 2 hours in a warm, draft-free place.

Heat enough oil for deep-frying in a large deep-sided heavy saucepan over medium to medium-high heat. To test whether the oil is hot enough, carefully drop in one of the *frittelle* – it should sizzle right away. Deep-fry the *frittelle* in batches for 5 minutes, until golden brown. Remove from the oil using a slotted spoon and drain on paper towels. Sprinkle with superfine sugar and serve immediately.

GNOCCHETTI FRITTI ALLA ANNARELLA
Sweet gnocchetti fritters

Made in the same way as fresh savory potato gnocchi, this dessert recipe is a family one. Again, as with the *frittelle*, these sweet morsels are at their best when served straight from pan to table.

✢ SERVES 4

1 lb 2 oz Italian tipo 00 flour or
  all-purpose flour
pinch of salt
5 large eggs, beaten
5 oz sugar
1 tablespoon pure vanilla extract
1 tablespoon baking powder
vegetable oil for deep-frying
confectioners' sugar for dusting

Put the flour in a bowl and make a well in the center. Add the salt, eggs, sugar, and vanilla extract. Mix well until smooth. Add the baking powder and continue mixing for about 10 minutes until the dough is smooth and elastic. Leave the dough to rest in the refrigerator for 1 hour.

To make the *gnocchetti*, knead the dough gently for a couple of minutes, then quickly roll out into finger-thick sausage-like strips. Cut up into 60 or so small pieces about 1 inch long, or the size of ordinary gnocchi.

Heat enough oil for deep-frying in a heavy saucepan over medium to medium-high heat. Add the *gnocchetti* a few at time, deep-frying for about 5 minutes, until golden. Remove from the pan using a slotted spoon and drain on paper towels. Continue frying in batches until all the dough has been used. Dust with confectioners' sugar and serve piping hot.

BABÀ
Yeast cake soaked in rum syrup

The babà arrived in Naples with the Bourbon court of the eighteenth century, the cooks in the royal household bringing the recipe with them from France. In their inimitable style, though, Neapolitans have made babà their own, and it is available from pastry shops all over the city both in the traditional large ring (kughelhopf) shape and baked in individual baba molds that look a little like flower pots. Babà are always well soaked in syrup, usually rum-based, although limoncello versions are becoming popular. Babà should be eaten on the same day it is made, or the next day at the latest.

⁙ SERVES 6–8

1 oz fresh yeast
12 oz tipo 00 flour or
   all-purpose flour
pinch of salt
9 oz butter
5 large eggs, beaten
1¹/₂ tablespoons sugar
¹/₄ cup light cream

For the syrup
3¹/₂ oz sugar
7 fl oz rum or limoncello

For the glacé icing (optional)
4 oz confectioners' sugar
3–4 tablespoons rum or limoncello

Mix the yeast with a little warm water. Add a few tablespoons of the flour and mix to a smooth paste. Leave to rise for about an hour in a warm place.

When the mixture has doubled in size, combine with the remaining flour, salt, butter, and eggs. Mix vigorously to a dough, kneading with your hands until it comes away from the sides of the bowl. Add the sugar and cream. Continue kneading for a few minutes, then transfer to a high-sided buttered babà mold. The dough should not come up past a third of the mold's height. Leave to rise again for about 2 hours in a dry, draft-free place. Bake in a preheated oven at 400°F (200°C) for 20 minutes, until golden.

In the meantime, make a syrup by bringing 1²/₃ cups water to a boil with the sugar and rum or limoncello. Remove the babà from the oven and pour over the syrup, allowing it to soak into the cake. Allow to cool.

If you like, you can drizzle a thin glacé icing over the top, letting it run down the sides but not cover the babà completely. To make the icing, put the confectioners' sugar in a bowl and mix in the rum (if you used the rum syrup) or limoncello (if you used limoncello) a tablespoon at a time until the icing is smooth and runny. Remember that the icing will set slightly once on the cake, but you do not want it to be so runny that it slides off completely. Drizzle the icing around the top of the cake so that it runs down the sides in "rivulets" and let set before serving.

FESTIVALS AND CELEBRATIONS

While it is true that the emphasis in the cuisine of Naples and surrounding Campania is not on desserts, there is definitely a love of sweet things that is perhaps not as prevalent in other parts of Italy. You can start and end your day with something sweet, whether it is bought from a bakery or *pasticceria*, or made at home. There are numerous sweet pastries to choose from, and special cakes and tarts associated with particular places, such as the *torta caprese*. Fruit appears in various forms, and dessert will often simply be a serving of fresh fruit such as citrus fruits, figs, peaches, apricots, or cherries. Use is also made of the region's abundance of nuts, such as almonds, chestnuts, and walnuts, in *torrone* (nougat) and other sweets such as *confetti* (sugared almonds), as well as biscuits, pastries, and cakes. And then, of course, there are the ice creams: *gelati*, *semifreddi*, *sorbetti*, *spumoni*, *ghiacciate* (syrup-flavored shaved ice), and *granite*. Ice cream and ices are a delight on a hot summer's day, and range from simple *gelati* flavored with the region's outstanding citrus fruits or pistachios, to the more elaborate *spumoni*, rich with nuts.

Many of Campania's most distinctive and well-known desserts and pastries, like some of the best-loved savory dishes, are traditionally linked with festivals and celebrations, or particular times of the year. *Carnevale*, Lent, Easter, Christmas, saints' days – where there is a celebration or special occasion, there is usually a pastry or dessert specially served to mark the event. A special chocolate cream, *sanguinaccio* (page 140), is eaten during carnival, for instance.

Pastiera napoletana (see pages 138–9) is eaten at Easter and has been for centuries; however, much further in the past this ricotta and wheat-grain cake was part of ceremonial offerings to spring, and in particular to the siren Parthenope. Parthenope has long been associated with Naple: it is said that following her failure to lure Odysseus onto the rocks of the Li Galli Islands off the Amalfi coast, she threw herself into the sea in despair and was washed up on the shore of the Bay of Naples from which the settlement of Naples eventually grew. The rich *pastiera napoletana* is usually served in thin slices for breakfast, over the Easter week.

Zeppole di San Giuseppe appear every year for the Feast of Saint Joseph on March 19th in their *bignè* (choux pastry) form, topped with custard cream and cherry jam. The other type of *zeppole*, made of a simpler dough, is usually served at Christmas. So, too, are the traditional spice biscuits *mostaccioli* and *roccocò* (see page 141).

Perhaps the most exuberant of all Neapolitan desserts are *struffoli* (see pages 154–5). Made to signify abundance and eaten at Christmas, these fritters are soaked in honey syrup and decorated freely with sprinkles, candied citron, and orange peel.

STRUFFOLI
Christmas fritters with honey and candied peel

These classic Christmas fritters symbolize abundance for Neapolitans. In a society where food was scarce and making a living from the land was difficult, *struffoli* were considered a symbol of good luck, as well as a food of celebration. Anyone who eats *struffoli* is supposed to enjoy a prosperous and plentiful year ahead.

⁙ SERVES 4

14 oz Italian tipo 00 flour or
  all-purpose flour
1 oz butter, roughly cubed
3 large eggs plus 3 yolks
1 tablespoon brandy
9 oz sugar
pinch of salt
grated zest of 1 lemon
grated zest of 1 orange
9 oz honey
5 oz orange and citron peel, finely
  chopped, plus extra, to decorate
sprinkles, to decorate
silver and gold dragees, to decorate
angelica and glacé cherries, halved,
  to decorate
vegetable oil for deep-frying

On a pastry board or in a large bowl, use a spatula to combine the flour with the butter, eggs, brandy, 1 tablespoon of the sugar, a pinch of salt, and the grated lemon and orange zest. Mix well and let sit in the refrigerator for about an hour. Roll out the pastry into very thin strips and cut into small pieces.

Heat the oil in a high-sided heavy saucepan over medium heat. To test whether the oil is hot enough for frying, fry a small piece of the *struffoli* dough first – it should sizzle right away. Deep-fry the *struffoli* for 5 minutes, a few at a time, until golden. Remove with a slotted spoon and drain on paper towels.

Put the honey and remaining sugar in a very large saucepan with $^1/_4$ cup water. Bring to a boil and continue boiling until the foam that forms on the top has disappeared completely and the honey has turned a light amber color. Add the *struffoli* and finely chopped candied peel. Stir over very gentle heat until they are all coated with the honey glaze.

Use a wooden spoon to turn out the *struffoli* onto a serving plate, and arrange into a pyramid, ring, or any shape you prefer. Decorate with the sprinkles, extra peel, silver and gold dragees, and small pieces of angelica and glacé cherries. To eat, simply break off individual *struffoli* with your fingers, and enjoy with a cup of fine-quality Neapolitan coffee.

INDEX

With many thanks to Manuela Barzan, Director of I.R.V.A.T. (Istituto per la Valorizzazione e la Tutela dei Prodotti Regionali), an association of provincial councils and chambers of commerce in Campania for the promotion of regional products on a global level.

First published in 2008 by
Interlink Books
An imprint of Interlink Publishing Group, Inc.
46 Crosby Street, Northampton, Massachusetts, 01060
www.interlinkbooks.com

1 3 5 7 9 10 8 6 4 2

ISBN 978 1 56656 724 4

PUBLISHING DIRECTOR: Rosemary Wilkinson
PROJECT EDITOR: Siobhán O'Connor, Lynne Saner
FOOD CONSULTANT: Hiltrud Schulz
TRANSLATION: I.R.V.A.T.
DESIGNER: Sue Rose, Casebourne Rose Design Associates
COVER DESIGN: Juliana Spear
RECIPE PHOTOGRAPHS: Frank Wieder
HOME ECONOMIST: Kate Moseley; ADDITIONAL PHOTO SHOOT: Wendy Sweetser
NAPLES PHOTOGRAPHY: Hannah Mornement

Printed and bound by Tien Wah Press, Malaysia

To request our 40-page full-color catalog,
please call us toll free at **1-800-238-LINK**,
visit our website at **www.interlinkbooks.com**,
or send us an email: **info@interlinkbooks.com**